THE GREAT THEMES OF SCRIPTURE:
NEW TESTAMENT

The Great Themes of Scripture

NEW TESTAMENT

Richard Rohr
and Joseph Martos

Nihil Obstat: Rev. Hilarion Kistner, O.F.M.
Rev. John J. Jennings

Imprimi Potest: Rev. Jeremy Harrington, O.F.M.
Provincial

Imprimatur: +James H. Garland, V.G.
Archdiocese of Cincinnati
November 13, 1987

The *nihil obstat* and *imprimatur* are a declaration that a book or pamphlet is considered to be free from doctrinal or moral error. It is not implied that those who have granted the *nihil obstat* and *imprimatur* agree with the contents, opinions or statements expressed.

Foreword

When I first gave the "Great Themes of Scripture" talks as a young priest in 1973, I little imagined how they would change my life, and apparently the lives of many others!

They changed mine because they were put on audiocassette—when not many Catholics were doing that yet (hard to believe!)—and therefore spread my message far beyond my original audience. But they changed my life in another way: Having my remarks made so public, I was sometimes forced to *believe* what I had now *said* about faith and the Word of God.

These talks led me on my own journey of faith—around much of the world—talking till I tired of my own voice, meeting countless Christians and communities, seeing sights and knowing sorrows that have further changed me, and now leading me to leave my beloved New Jerusalem in Cincinnati for a new venture in New Mexico.

I would rather have been like Terah, the father of Abraham, and stopped at more familiar Haran (Genesis 11:31), but I had unfortunately *talked* about the complete journey to Canaan. I would much rather have been like Aaron, the priest who himself formed the golden calf (Exodus 32:4), but I had unawares spoken of Moses, who railed at idolatry and was tortured with dissatisfaction. I could easier have been "a nice priest" (like my mother wanted), but now I had heard of Isaiah, Jeremiah, Amos and John the Baptist—from my own mouth on audiocassette! I could have quite easily been a "good" Christian, a pious charismatic, a dedicated minister of the system, but I had unthinkingly talked about—and talked to—this Jesus Man. I am trapped, even if not yet converted. My words returned again and again to condemn and console me.

There are two people that I must particularly "blame" for these tapes-now-become-book: First, Sister Pat Brockman, O.S.U., who talked me into taping them against my better judgment and my Franciscan humility. She was convinced that others might like to hear them and, with her loving optimism, convinced the wary staff at St. Anthony Messenger of the same. Further, her energetic realism said that we needed to make money for the new youth ministry that we were then involved in (which was eventually to become the New Jerusalem Community). Second, I must blame Father Jeremy Harrington, O.F.M., then editor of *St. Anthony Messenger* and now our most appreciated Provincial. He has the grace to affirm and believe in just about any friar! And so he did, and still does, with me and many others. Ah, the peril of loving friends!

There is also someone I must now thank—for taking my style of expression, that somehow seems to work as a speaking style, and making it into a readable prose style: I congratulate Joe Martos. He did what I was convinced was impossible. By the metamorphosis of love, patience (oh, so much!), and skill, he took my-spoken-words-trying-to-be-God's-Word and made them into a much better written word—which is still God's and mine, but also Joe's. And that is exactly what Scripture should be! Umm, the loves of perilous friends!

To be honest, I would probably say a lot of this differently now. Then I was young, convicted, surrounded by hope and easy joy. These are the necessary beginning words of the evangelist. I am happy I said them. Now I am older, chastened by failures, rejections, human suffering, study and the sophistications and nuances of supposed experience.

Do I now know more or less? Were these words adequate, or am I saying it better now? Which naivete is preferred, first or second? I am really not sure, and needn't be. I am just very grateful that I am "trapped" in these effusions of youthful Good News by the miracle of technology that Jesus and Paul never had. I wish they had, but for now I will content myself with wishing that Jesus and Paul, and all the holy crowd, will be able to speak to you through these sounds on paper, this desire to communicate on the part of God, Richard and Joe.

I think God Himself/Herself would agree that James Carroll's evaluation of his own words apply aptly to this book as well: "Most of it is heresy, some of it is absurd, and all of it is true."

Richard Rohr, O.F.M.
March 20, 1987
Center for Action and Contemplation
Albuquerque, New Mexico

Preface

This book is a work of collaboration. Like a Gilbert and Sullivan operetta or a Rodgers and Hammerstein musical, it is the combined effort of two persons. Each has his own special gifts, his own unique talents.

Richard's special gift is inspired and inspiring speaking. He has been recognized for this by being invited to preach and teach around the world, and by making a number of cassette recordings which have sold thousands of copies.

My own unique talent is clear and organized writing. People tell me that my first book really helped them understand the history of the Catholic sacraments even though they were not theologians. In my second book I was able to pull together information from psychology, sociology, history, theology and spirituality in order to present a contemporary evaluation of the sacraments in the life of the Church.

Readers who have listened to Richard Rohr's cassette series *The Great Themes of Scripture* will know where the inspiration for this book comes from. When I first undertook the task of editing those tapes to put them into print, I was hoping to smooth out the grammar here and there, introduce paragraphing to the continuous flow of Richard's ideas, and make as few alterations as possible. As my work progressed, however, it became clear that Richard's charismatic delivery could not be easily transcribed onto the printed page. I knew that I would have to add my own creative talent as a writer to his gift for spontaneous speaking if his ideas were to reach the wider audience who would benefit from having those cassettes in book form.

It has been a rewarding collaboration. Not only has Richard been an inspiration to me and a patient supporter of this project, but other members of the New Jerusalem Community in Cincinnati have also given of their time and talent in the earlier stages of this work. I would especially like to thank Walt Bassett for his practical advice and technical assistance and Sister Pat Brockman for the work she did on an earlier typescript of *The Great Themes*.

If our collaborative effort has been successful, this book will appear to be all of a piece with each chapter part of a unified whole. Readers may wonder which of us contributed what to the finished work. And if I would acknowledge that the words are often mine, I must always admit that the music is Richard's.

Joseph Martos

Contents

Introduction   1

CHAPTER ONE
Matthew's Good News: The Reign of God!   3

CHAPTER TWO
Mark and John's Good News: Jesus Is Lord!   35

CHAPTER THREE
Luke and Acts: The Gift of the Spirit   71

CHAPTER FOUR
Mary, Prayer and the Church. Let It Be!   99

CHAPTER FIVE
Paul: A New Creation   129

CHAPTER SIX
Apocalypse: The New Jerusalem   155

CONCLUSION
Our New Jerusalem: A Modern Faith Journey   165

Introduction

The great themes of the New Testament build on those of the Old Testament, and yet they go beyond them. The New Testament is sometimes called the New Covenant, signifying a new relationship between humanity and God. Yet, as we have already seen in the previous volume, it was not God who changed. It is not as though God decided to let people get along with an old-model covenant until he was good and ready to give them a new one. Rather, it is human beings who changed. The people of Israel had to grow in their understanding of God and the salvation God promised them. Human faith had to develop to the point where people could enter into a new relationship, a new covenant with the God who had always loved them unconditionally. The New Testament is the story of that new relationship.

From the viewpoint of salvation history, the New Testament is the completion and the culmination of the Old. In terms of length, it is only a small portion of the entire Bible, and yet it is that portion which brings it all together. The history of God's salvation of the human race is completed in the story of Jesus, whose name means "Yahweh saves." All the words of the Bible lead to and culminate in the incarnate Word, which is Christ the Lord.

What we see in Jesus is the personification of God's salvation. The life of Jesus dramatizes what God was always doing in the life of Israel, what God is always doing in every human life, and what God will always be doing in the life of

1

the Church. In Jesus, God's saving love is clearly seen as unconditional, working to redeem every person and every situation, even to the point of ultimate self-sacrifice, symbolized in the crucifixion. But in Jesus too, God's saving power is clearly seen as unlimited, both in the stories of his miracles and in the overwhelmingly significant event of his resurrection.

Throughout the chapters* of this book we will look at the many ways these salvation themes are proclaimed by the various authors and literary styles of the New Testament.

---

* The talks on which the chapters in this book are based were given in 1973.

CHAPTER ONE

Matthew's Good News: The Reign of God!

The New Testament in its present form consists of 27 books in four main literary genres or styles: *gospel, acts, epistle* and *apocalyptic*. As we shall see, however, the present appearance of these books does not always represent their original shape. Nor does it represent the order in which they were originally composed.

The gospels are generally divided into the "synoptics" (from Greek words meaning "one view," since they seem to share a single perspective in the way they are written) and the gospel of John (which is written from a very different perspective). The Book of Acts continues the gospel genre past the ministry of Jesus and into the activities of the early apostles and blends it with the literary genre of Church history. The epistles range from somewhat lengthy theological reflections to rather brief practical letters. And the Book of the Apocalypse, or Revelation, is written in a very prophetic style, reminiscent of some portions of the Old Testament.

The Meaning of the Gospels

The four gospels in the New Testament are unique. There is nothing else quite like them in the world of religious or secular literature. They are similar in some respects to the stories of Old Testament heroes in which the meaning of events is more important than the details. But they are different inasmuch as

3

they try to say not who Jesus *was*, but who he *is*.

The gospels are testimonials of faith in the living, risen Jesus, written by believers for other believers. They were never meant to convince nonbelievers of the divinity of Christ, for example, although they were later used for that. They were attempts to explain more fully to those who already put their faith in Jesus who it is that they are trusting.

We know from modern research that the good news about Jesus was actually passed along by word of mouth for many years before it got written down. The gospels which were eventually recognized as sacred scripture by the early Christians were not composed and edited till decades after Jesus' life in Palestine. Although they bear the names of Matthew, Mark, Luke and John, scholars are not all convinced that they were actually written by the apostles and disciples mentioned in the New Testament. For our purposes we can suppose that they were, but we must remember that authorship in ancient times was less precise than it is today. It is very likely that these four documents stand on the authority of those very early witnesses who knew Jesus, or who knew those who knew Jesus.

But whoever actually wrote the gospels, one thing is very certain: They are not intended as biographies of Jesus or as news accounts of some sort. They were not meant to be accurate in every detail, living up to the standards of modern history and journalism. People who believe that the Bible must live up to modern conceptions of literal truth are known as biblical literalists or fundamentalists. They mistakenly expect ancient literature to be measured by the standards of modern realism.

But what was real for people in ancient times was not limited to what could be seen or heard. What was really real for them could be the experience of Christ's presence, or of the Spirit's power, or of the Father's love. And so the ancient authors crafted their stories in ways which would awaken or explain those experiences for their readers. Likewise, what was important to the ancients was not the details which often fascinate us but the religious meaning which shines through all the details. With that in mind, the biblical writers often adapted what they received from their sources to their own purposes or to the needs of their own particular audiences.

4

Some of the evangelists knew of "gospels" which had been written before them. Matthew, Mark and Luke contain a fair amount of similar material, so undoubtedly someone borrowed from someone else. Today we might call that plagiarism, but these authors saw the good news about Jesus as the common heritage of the Christian community.

What's more, in borrowing stories from each other they sometimes changed the details to fit their emphasis, and they saw nothing wrong with that either. For example, all four gospels have a story about the baptism of Jesus by John, but all four tell it slightly differently. Yet none of the gospel writers suggests that the others are wrong because they arrange the details differently. So today, if we would compare the four and ask which author is telling the truth and which is lying, we would betray that we had a much more limited understanding of truth than the evangelists.

The beauty of the gospels, and indeed of all the scriptures, is this: If read with reverence and openness to the Lord, they can be taken either literally or symbolically. Someone of simple faith without much education can read the story of the annunciation, believe that an angel literally appeared to a young maiden, and marvel at Mary's willingness to serve the Lord. But someone else from a more sophisticated background can read the same story, take the angel as symbolizing a word that came to Mary as she meditated on God's actions in her life, and marvel at her continuous readiness to serve the Lord. We do not know which of these two interpretations is more accurate; nor do we need to. In either interpretation it is obvious that its religious meaning is the same.

There is a scene in the Gospel According to Matthew which is a window into the world of the evangelist. In chapter 16 Peter expresses his belief that Jesus is the anointed Son of God, which prompts Jesus to tell him, "You are a happy man, for this was not revealed to you by any human being but by my Father!" Peter and the apostles first knew Jesus as a man, just as other people did. But then at some point they went beyond what human eyes could see to what could be seen only with the eyes of faith. What they saw was good news to them, and so when they told others about it, it was called simply that. The original word for gospel literally means "good news."

What the gospels are about, therefore, is precisely that good news. It is not something that could have been caught on film if movie cameras had been around then. It is not something that could be scientifically measured or impartially observed. It is a wisdom that can only be experienced *after* the "leap of faith."

The gospels, in a sense, are an attempt to portray the faith of one generation of Christians to the next generation of Christians. This cannot be done directly, but only through stories and pictures. To overanalyze the stories or pictures, therefore, is to miss the point. The point is something that goes beyond what eyes can see and ears can hear. The point is good news that cannot be argued logically or proven rationally. It can only be experienced—received as gift and accepted in faith.

Another way to think about the meaning of the gospels is in terms of a relationship. Christians who had never seen Jesus in the flesh but who had only walked with him in the Spirit needed to know how to relate to the risen Lord. They needed to know how to relate to him personally, as savior and healer and forgiver of their sins. The gospel stories gave them models of how they might, like the blind or sick or crippled who met Jesus in the flesh, reach out to him in faith and be touched by him.

This next generation of Christians also needed to know how to relate to the risen Lord "in the body," that is, in the community of believers. For years the sayings and the parables of Jesus had been passed along by word of mouth to meet this need, but now the oral tradition passed into a written form as the good news of how to live in Christ, in the body of the Lord, filled with his Spirit.

These early Christian documents, therefore, are anything but documentaries. They are not about the life of Jesus *then;* they are about life with Jesus *now.* They are written *by* people of faith *for* people of faith. They describe not so much past events but a present person and contemporary relationships.

If in reading the gospels we do not come into the presence of Jesus, we are not reading them correctly. If in reading the gospels we do not hear Jesus speaking to our contemporary situation, we are missing their meaning. If in reading the gospels

6

we do not enter and reenter into a relationship with the risen Lord, we are not experiencing their power.

It is the power of the gospels which made them good news for the Christians of the first century. It is the inspiration of the gospels which led the early Church to acknowledge them as sacred scripture.

Why the 'Reign of God' Is Good News

There is a very ancient tradition that Matthew is the oldest of the four gospels. This refers, however, to an earlier version of Matthew than our Gospel According to Matthew.

Modern scripture scholars believe that Matthew's original gospel was written in Aramaic (the language of Palestine in the time of Jesus) and that it was later translated into Greek and combined with other materials by an unknown Christian of the first century. This longer gospel was probably written around 80 A.D., give or take five or 10 years, judging by the kinds of evidence which researchers use to date ancient documents.

We no longer have the Aramaic gospel, but scholars judge that this earlier document had to exist as a primary source for the later document, which we call the Gospel According to Matthew. Because the first biblical researchers to propose this theory were German, the Aramaic gospel is referred to as the "Q document" for *Quelle*, which means "source" in German.

Internal evidence suggests that the later Greek gospel was composed for a community of Christians of Jewish descent. Matthew makes numerous references to Old Testament prophesies, shows concern for the requirements of the Law and portrays Jesus in many ways as a new Moses—none of which would have made sense to non-Jewish believers in Jesus.

The main theme which runs through Matthew's gospel is also very Jewish, although Jesus' use of it is quite original. The theme is that of the "kingdom of God," the "kingdom of heaven," or the "reign of God"; all three phrases translate the same idea, the same reality, the same experience.

The idea goes back to the ancient period of the judges when the Israelites had no earthly king because only Yahweh ruled over all 12 tribes. When Saul and David were anointed, it was with the understanding that Yahweh was the only Lord of the kings of Israel, and that their kingdom was ultimately his. But the Israelites eventually turned away from living under Yahweh's lordship and their earthly kingdom was destroyed. The prophets urged the people to return to Yahweh's rule, and many hoped for the coming of the reign of God in the form of a new earthly kingdom. Finally the wisdom writers expanded the idea of God's rule even further, seeing Yahweh as the creator and sustainer of the universe.

Jesus began his public ministry with the announcement of the coming of God's kingdom—an old idea to which he gave added meaning. Matthew quotes Jesus as saying, "Repent! The kingdom of heaven is near" (Matthew 4:17). A few lines later he says that Jesus went all around Galilee "proclaiming the good news of the kingdom and curing all kinds of sickness and disease among the people" (Matthew 4:23).

When we hear of repentance we often have visions of hair shirts, flagellation and other medieval penances—all of them undoubtedly bad news! But the biblical idea of repentance, originating with the prophets, was more like a change of heart, a turning around, a new attitude. The Greek word *metanoia* means a transformation of one's whole mentality. So here Jesus is prophetically telling his listeners to do a mental turnaround, to "repent."

But to turn *from* what *to* what? Again Jesus' message is very prophetic: to turn from self-centeredness and self-reliance to concern for others and trust in God. The biblical theme of absolute faith and total reliance on God always means letting go, surrendering to the Lord. Repentance in the Bible always means turning from self to God, from focusing on our own needs and wants to focusing on the Lord. When we do that, when we let go of lesser gods and let God be our only Lord, we enter into his kingdom. The reign of God begins when we let God begin to reign in our hearts.

And so the kingdom of heaven is near. The reign of God is always close at hand. It is as near as our willingness to recognize our inability to save ourselves and to surrender to God as our savior. It is as close as our readiness to look to the Lord rather than to other things for our happiness. We enter into it as soon as we stop being closed in on ourselves and start opening up to the freedom of self-forgetfulness.

So the news about the reign of God is good, first of all, because it proclaims that God is with us. When we lose ourselves enough to find the Lord, we discover not only his presence but also his love and his power. Matthew applies the prophetic name Emmanuel (meaning "God is with us") to Jesus (Matthew 1:23), but Jesus here is saying that God is with each and every one of us. All we need to do is repent, to turn and face God, to recognize God's presence.

The news of the reign of God is good, secondly, because it proclaims that God loves us. He loves us unconditionally with an infinite love that we could never merit. Matthew says that the Father recognized Jesus as his beloved Son (Matthew 3:17), but if God always loves with an infinite love, then surely he cannot love us any less than he loves Jesus. He loves all his sons and daughters unconditionally.

Third, the news of the reign of God is good because it means that God's power is with us. Matthew links Jesus' proclamation of the kingdom to his healing of the people's illnesses (Matthew 4:23), but Jesus himself says that his followers should be able to do as much as he does (Matthew 17:20).

So when Jesus announces the good news that God's kingdom is *near*, he is saying that, except for our lack of repentance, the kingdom is *here*. It is as close as our recognition of God's presence, love and power in our lives.

There is a place in Luke's gospel where Jesus spells this out more clearly:

> Asked by the Pharisees when the kingdom of God was to come, he gave them this answer, "The coming of the kingdom of God does not admit of observation, and there will be no one to say, 'Look, it is here! Look, it is there!' For look, the kingdom of God is among you." (Luke 17:20-21 JB)

Some older translations say instead, "the kingdom of God is within you." The Greek words can be translated either way, and both translations are true in their own way. Repentance is something that takes place within; it is a change of heart, a conversion of one's whole mentality. In a very real sense, the kingdom begins within us.

But in another, equally real sense, the kingdom takes place among us. Living in the kingdom is a matter of living in right relationship, and relationships exist only between and among people. Living in right relationship with God means letting God be Lord, letting God be first, letting God's love reign in our hearts. But if we are living in God's love, then living with others means loving them the same way God loves us (Matthew 5:43-48). Living in right relationship with others means we are concerned for their welfare and go out to meet their needs, just as Jesus did. And living in relationships of mutual self-giving with others means we make God's kingdom something real in this world, even though it is not a worldly kingdom. Nevertheless, it is a reality which is both personal and public, both private and corporate.

Scripture scholars sometimes point out that Jesus preached the good news of the kingdom, but the early Christians preached the good news of Jesus. Mark, for a very clear example, begins with the words, "The beginning of the good news of Jesus Christ, the Son of God" (Mark 1:1).

These two versions of the good news can appear to be in opposition, until we remember that for the earliest Christians the coming of the kingdom coincided with the coming of Jesus. The kingdom began to be realized on earth with Jesus' living in perfect sonship to the Father, and with his living in perfect relationship to others. He lived completely under the reign of God, loving others with divine love, healing them with divine power. For the gospel writers, therefore, Jesus was the living example of what he had proclaimed about the kingdom.

An Overview of Matthew

Matthew's gospel is thus both the good news of the coming of Jesus and the good news of the coming of the kingdom. His story unfolds as a drama which progresses through a series of stages, each with its own revelation about the life of Jesus and the nature of the kingdom.

Chapters 3 and 4 begin the drama with the baptism of Jesus and his initial proclamation of the kingdom. In chapters 5 through 7 Jesus gives the Sermon on the Mount, his first and major teaching about living in the kingdom. Then chapters 8 and 9 demonstrate the power of the kingdom. Just as Moses showed God's power in the 10 plagues through which the Hebrews were freed from Egypt, now Jesus through God's power liberates his people from sickness and disease.

In chapter 10 Jesus tells the 12 apostles what to do and what to expect when he sends them out to announce the coming of the kingdom. In chapters 11 and 12 opposition to Jesus begins to show itself, but Jesus tells his disciples how to overcome obstacles to the kingdom.

Chapter 13 contains parables about the kingdom which explain its elusive nature. Those who are living in the kingdom know very well what the parables are about; those who have not entered into it find their meaning puzzling. The kingdom is a "this-world" reality, to be brought to fulfillment by God.

Chapters 14 through 17 show the kingdom beginning to be realized: A community is gathering around Jesus. He feeds the people through the multiplication of loaves and fishes. His disciples recognize him as the messiah, and he is transfigured with Moses and Elijah on the mountain. At the same time, however, Jesus is beginning to run into opposition from the leaders of the Jewish religion.

In Chapter 18 we hear Jesus telling his followers how to live together in the kingdom. In a way, he is explaining what the Church is all about. It is a means to the kingdom, but it is not the kingdom itself. This has often been forgotten.

Beginning with chapter 19 and going on through chapter

23 we see the tension building between the kingdom of heaven and the kingdom of this world. Jesus is jubilantly welcomed into Jerusalem by the common people, but his teaching is resisted by the religious officials in the temple. So chapters 24 and 25 predict the downfall of religious formalism and the final triumph of the kingdom. The destruction of Jerusalem symbolizes the end of the world and the beginning of the messianic era.

In chapters 26 and 28 the kingdom reality is finally spread across the earth through the suffering, death and raising up of Jesus. The good news of the kingdom is vindicated by God in the resurrection of the one who trusted in God completely and offered himself up fully to the Father in service of others.

The end of the gospel is therefore the beginning of the good news that life in the kingdom has become available to all. The messiah of the Jews has become the savior of all the nations of the world. By moving through the apparent defeat of death to the glorious victory of resurrection, Jesus becomes the ultimate example of living in the kingdom. The kingdom is wherever God's truth and this world meet and coincide. It is not describing heaven or the spread of the Church as such.

The divine plan of salvation has now become completely revealed. The promised land—which Abraham imagined to be Canaan and which each succeeding Jewish generation believed lay just ahead of them—has finally been entered into by Jesus the Christ, Jesus the Messiah. Instead of being conquered, he is the conqueror. Instead of being victim, he is victorious. But he is not the last; he is the first, and the one who shows the way. The final outcome of our lives will be the same as his, if like him we seek to live fully in the kingdom, to live God's truth in this world. And that's good news. (But it's also bad news for those who have put their hope in this world's beliefs and rewards.)

The Infancy Narrative

We have not yet mentioned the first two chapters of the Gospel According to Matthew. Although these chapters speak about Jesus, they do not form part of the drama of the coming of the kingdom. Instead, they are a sort of preface to the main development in the book, and so they need to be treated separately. We find a similar preface in Luke's gospel.

We have already seen how the gospels are not biographies of Jesus but statements of faith written by and for the early Christian community. This is especially true of these special sections of Matthew and Luke which we call the infancy narratives. They are not found in Mark and John, nor is any mention of Jesus' birth made in the earliest preaching of the good news, as reflected in the Acts of the Apostles. (See, for example, the speech of Peter in Acts 2:22-36.)

In the infancy narratives there is much more theology than biography, much more myth than history. In this respect they are similar to the creation stories in Genesis. In the absence of scientific information about the beginning of the world, the religious imagination describes the way the world is right now through a story set at the beginning of time. Every religious culture has always done this, and the Jews were no exception. In the same way, therefore, without concrete biographical information about the birth of Jesus, early Christian theologians (if we might call them that) developed stories about his birth which expressed their present understanding of him *after* the resurrection.

Ancient peoples understood this mythic mode of expressing religious truth much more readily than we do. It is we who often misunderstand these documents by assuming that they mean what we take them to mean as we read them in our culture 20 centuries after they were written. The result is biblical fundamentalism, a naive and literal interpretation of the scripture which is based on the mistake of reading ancient documents with a modern mentality. To find the meaning of the Bible, however, we often have to first understand it as ancient writing before we can appreciate it as eternal Word.

An excellent example of this is the genealogy of Jesus with which Matthew opens chapter 1. Upon close inspection, it is a contrived and symbolic tracing of Jesus' ancestry. Historically, there must have been many more generations from Abraham to Jesus than the ones which are mentioned. Biblically, the ones which are mentioned here do not correspond exactly

to the generations which are found in the Old Testament. So
the author has obviously arranged the names in order to make
a theological statement—in fact, a number of them.

For instance, Matthew traces the lineage of Jesus to David
and Abraham (Matthew 1:1). Why these two? Because if Jesus
is the messiah, then he must be of the house of David. Many
Jews were expecting the messiah to be of David's royal line.
Likewise, if Jesus is the messiah, he must be an Israelite, a son
of Abraham. Also, Jesus is a man of truth who trusts totally in
the Father; and so Abraham, the great man of faith, is his
ancestor.

You notice that Matthew gives three sets of 14 generations
in his genealogy. Fourteen (or twice seven) was a symbolic
number of fulfillment for the Jews. Thus the lists, artificially
constructed to contain 14 generations each, say symbolically that
the time was fulfilled for the messiah to come. But count the
names. Matthew says in verse 17 that each list has 14 names,
but the last one has only 13. Why? It is his way of saying that
the immediate father of Jesus was not Joseph but the Holy Spirit;
God himself is the 14th and immediate ancestor of Jesus. He
says it here by omission, as it were, in a way that the ancient
mind could recognize and appreciate. He says the same thing
straightforwardly in the very next verse:

> This is how Jesus Christ came to be born. His mother
> Mary was betrothed to Joseph, but before they came
> to live together she was found to be with child
> through the Holy Spirit. (Matthew 1:18)

In Luke's gospel an angel appears to Mary to announce
the birth of Christ; in Matthew, an angel speaks to Joseph in a
dream. In ancient literature the presence of an angel signifies
the sacredness of a place or an event; the angel manifests the
presence and power of God in a visible way. It is quite probable
that Matthew and Luke introduce an angel as a literary way of
symbolizing the close connection between Jesus and the Father.
It is not so much a statement about the birth of Jesus as it is a
statement about the *person* of Jesus.

A few lines later in Matthew we read about the magi,

who appear in none of the other gospels. If we scrutinize this story the way that scripture scholars do, we can see that it is more theological than historical in nature. (But even common sense wonders why, if the holy family had really been given such great wealth at the birth of Jesus, Joseph didn't retire for life!) Why would Matthew have either constructed this story or (which is more likely) included in his gospel this story which he found in his first-century Christian community?

One of the hard issues which the earliest Christians (who were all Jews) had to face was that gentiles were coming to know Jesus and accept him as their Lord. It seems likely, then, that through this story of wise men from foreign lands acknowledging Jesus as the messiah, Matthew is depicting the growing understanding in the Church that Jesus did not come just for the sake of the Jews. He is thus teaching a later truth through a story about an earlier event: that Jesus is the savior not only of the chosen people but of all people.

Although we imagine the magi as kings, Matthew depicts them as astrologers and scientists, as if to say that the wisdom of the nations is leading them to Jesus. And although we usually speak of three of them, the story does not actually say how many there were. It docs, however, mention three gifts, and from this Christians in later ages found it natural to imagine one person for each gift. As this story has continued to be embellished in later centuries, we get some insight into how religious imagination works: It expresses itself in symbols which reflect its understanding of what is true and real.

The last major episode in Matthew's infancy narrative is the flight of the holy family to Egypt. Here again we have two very strong clues that this is a theological story and not history in the modern sense. Geographically, the Negev desert is difficult enough to cross in a modern land rover; a man and a woman with a baby would never have made it across on foot. Historically, it is very doubtful that Herod ever massacred all the infants in Bethlehem. We can say this with some certainty because the Jewish historian Josephus, who hated Herod and dug up all the dirt he could on him, never mentions it.

Why then this theological story? What point is it making? We have to figure it out through scholarship, but to Matthew's

Jewish audience the meaning would have been obvious. They understood Jesus as the new Moses—in fact, one even greater than Moses. But Moses was saved from Pharaoh's slaughter of the Hebrew children (Exodus 1:15—2:9). In parallel fashion, then, Jesus is rescued from Herod's slaughter of the innocents. Also, Moses came out of Egypt with the Israelites. So, by depicting Jesus as coming out of Egypt after the death of Herod, Matthew is again portraying Jesus as another Moses.

All through the infancy narrative, and then with less frequency throught the rest of this gospel, Matthew makes reference to Old Testament texts, usually introducing them with a phrase such as, "This was to fulfill what the prophet wrote." Obviously Matthew was doing this for his Jewish audience, who was familiar with these texts. The references would not have rung a bell with gentile converts at all, however.

Most of us are like those gentile converts. We did not grow up Jewish. And so when we see the gospel saying that something was done to fulfill a prophesy, we get the impression that a prophesy is some sort of prediction. Yet, if we make the effort to take a look at those Old Testament texts, we discover very quickly that few of them are predictions in the modern sense of that term.

Once again we have to see what Matthew was doing from a Jewish perspective in order to understand it correctly. For the Jews, any text in the Bible was a word from God. It therefore spoke the truth for all ages. Take the commandments, for example. Each of them was considered a word from God, and so any time a person obeyed the commandment, they fulfilled the word of God.

The prophets, as we have seen, also spoke God's word. They called for repentance, they announced destruction, they offered consolation. But in a broader sense, *any* scriptural text was prophetic since prophesying simply means speaking God's word. To the Jewish mind, then, whenever people *lived according to* what was said by a prophet or commandment or proverb or psalm, they were "fulfilling" the word of God.

For Matthew's Jewish Christians, it was important that Jesus be seen as someone who fulfilled the scriptures. It is not as though Matthew was expecting them (or us) to believe that the authors of the Old Testament wrote those texts with the messiah in mind. Rather, he is showing again and again, that since Jesus is the messiah, the perfect Son of the Father, he fulfilled the scriptures in all that he did.

Scenes From Matthew's Gospel

As we saw at the beginning of this chapter, the gospels are composite works—that is, their final authors or editors composed the gospels out of various stories and accounts which had already been circulating in the Christian community for many years. Besides this oral tradition, there was also a growing written tradition which consisted of collections of sayings, parables or miracles of Jesus, and perhaps accounts of the passion. Each of the evangelists sewed together these pieces of tradition into a finished work with more or less artistry. Mark comes off very much like a patchwork quilt; each of his little sections is joined to the next with a simple conjunction like *and* or *but* in the original Greek. John's gospel is more like a tapestry and perhaps the closest of the four to an original work of art. Luke and Matthew are artistically arranged collections, built around a basic theme, such as the kingdom of God.

But the fact remains that the gospels contain numerous sayings and incidents, each of which could be the subject of a commentary or sermon. Faced with such a wealth of possibilities, we can focus on only a few of the major ones in this chapter and the ones to come.

Temptation in the Desert

The event which is a prelude to the public ministry of Jesus in each of the gospels is his baptism in the Jordan by John. Here Jesus receives the spirit of God in a special way, his sonship is affirmed, and he accepts the call to preach the kingdom. Immediately after Jesus says his yes to God, there follows the "Temptation in the Desert." It is a time of purification, a facing of the temptations that every disciple will have to also face.

It's so human. It's just like us—promising to do something big and then we're suddenly wondering what we've gotten ourselves into! Jesus' temptations help him to clarify what his Father wants him to do. Likewise, they help us to understand the nature of his mission.

In the first temptation the devil puts some stones in front of Jesus and says, "If you are the son of God, tell these stones to turn into bread" (Matthew 4:2). He is saying, in effect, "Feed your human hunger and be satisfied." Now that's a very real temptation for all of us. We are often tempted to think that by filling ourselves up with what the world has to offer, we will find happiness.

But there is also a social dimension to this temptation. When we who call ourselves the sons and daughters of God look around and see the poor and starving of the world, we are tempted to believe that feeding and clothing them is all we need to do to help them. Both our conscience and our critics suggest that social programs will satisfy the starving of the world, and as children of God we feel a messianic urge to save them by giving them food. We should by all means give them bread, but it is "not by bread *alone*" that they will be satisfied (Matthew 4:4).

Jesus' reply does not deny the reality and demands of physical hunger. Surely he himself was feeling hungry after 40 days of fasting in the desert. But his answer points beyond physical needs to the deeper spiritual hunger which must be met if the human desire for salvation is to be ultimately satisfied. So even though we cannot deny the importance of food, clothing and shelter, Christ reminds us that, in the end, those things do not answer our needs. They are not eternal. They are not what life is all about. They are not what gives us meaning. What gives us meaning is every word of love that God speaks in our hearts. And we give meaning to the lives of others *both* by bread *and* by every word of love we speak to them.

Satan next takes Jesus to the top of a tower, telling him to jump off and let angels do the work of rescuing him. The temptation here, for Jesus and for us as well, is to play religious salvation games. It's the temptation to a false trust in religiosity, to cheap grace, to "the comfortable pew." If we give in to this temptation, our love is not for God, but for our own religious ingenuity and observances.

But that is not the message of the Bible. And so Jesus

18

answers in the words of scripture, "You must not put the Lord your God to the test" (Matthew 4:7). The divine plan is one which involves personal participation, listening for and responding to the call to faith. It is not some type of magic. It is a much slower process, the only truly human process, the only one which redeems and transforms us completely. Any other change would only be external and mechanical. It would not respect our humanity. And so it is not God's way of perfect salvation.

Finally the devil shows Jesus the kingdoms of the world, offering them all to him if he will renounce his faith in the Father. In a sense, this scene is a repeat of the temptation of the Israelites in the desert after they escaped from Egypt. Time and again they fell into the trap of wishing for the security of slavery, of giving up the sometimes scary freedom of trusting in God. This is our temptation, too, when we think we can find our security and prestige in the systems and institutions of the world instead of in God's kingdom.

What Israel did wrong, however, Jesus now does right. He tells the tempter to stop trying to dissuade him, because "You must worship the Lord your God, and serve him alone" (Matthew 4:10). So Jesus will not turn from the path which the Father has shown him. He will be obedient even in the desert, even when all the familiar landmarks are gone, even when it is so inviting to turn back. Thus Matthew's Jesus is not only a new Moses but also a new Israel; he is the son of God who fulfills all that the Israelites were called to be as sons and daughters of Yahweh.

Calling of the First Disciples

Soon after this testing of his own sonship, Jesus begins to invite others to join him in living fully in the Father's kingdom. He announces to all that the reign of God is readily available, but he also gives a special invitation to those who would learn from him how to be a child of God as fully as he is. Matthew describes this in the scene of the "Calling of the First Disciples."

It looks so perfectly simple. Jesus walks up to two fishermen on the shore and asks them to drop their nets and follow him; immediately Simon Peter and his brother Andrew become the first disciples. Then he gives the same invitation to James and John, and they too leave their boats and follow Jesus (Matthew 4:18-22).

When we start thinking about this scene, however, we realize that there is something very improbable about it. Unless people were quite different then from the way they are today, why should we believe that four solid citizens of Galilee would suddenly abandon their business to go off with a stranger who had just wandered in from the desert? Obviously Matthew is not reporting history here but teaching theology, instructing his readers on the meaning of discipleship. He is writing about Peter, Andrew, James and John, but he is talking about following the Lord.

Once we see the story in that light, we can hear what Matthew is saying. He is telling his readers that the call of the Lord brooks no delay. Once we know in our hearts that we should be disciples of Jesus, nothing should hold us back. Practical concerns cannot come first. Family ties cannot be given preference. All those are nets which entangle us in other preoccupations. The Lord asks us to drop our nets and follow him.

There was a time when Catholics generally thought that answering the call of God meant going to a seminary or a convent. Modern scripture scholarship assures us, however, that this and other gospel teachings on discipleship were meant for the whole Christian community, not just for a select few. According to Matthew and the other evangelists, then, being a Christian is the same as being a disciple of Christ. Following the Lord is the vocation of everyone, not just priests and nuns.

But what is Christ inviting his disciples to do? The last verses of chapter 4 give us Matthew's answer. Jesus goes about proclaiming the good news of the kingdom and healing people through the power of God that is within him. The call to follow Jesus is thus an invitation to live in the same space where Jesus lives, under the reign of the Father, filled with his power and using it to overcome the evils of the world. The miracles that Jesus works symbolize the amazing things that start to happen when people realize and respond to God's power of salvation. This is truly good news!

Sermon on the Mount

The first readers of Matthew's gospel may have been as eager as Peter, Andrew, James and John to heed the call to discipleship, but unlike the very first disciples they did not have Jesus to teach them concretely and practically what discipleship means in their everyday lives. So in the next long section of his gospel, which tradition has named the "Sermon on the Mount," Matthew has collected many teachings of Jesus about what it means to live kingdom values in this world. In the gospel discourse it looks like one long sermon, but it is actually a summary of many things that Jesus must have said at various times throughout his ministry.

Matthew has two reasons for putting all of this material in one place. The first is his literary concern to draw together many teachings of the Lord into one manageable discourse. The second is his theological concern to portray Jesus as the new Moses. Luke's gospel contains some of this same material in a sermon Jesus preaches in a field (see Luke 6:20-49). But for Matthew's Jewish community, these teachings of Jesus are their new Torah, their new way of life. So Matthew shows Jesus proclaiming the Law of Christ from a mountaintop, paralleling the way that Moses brought the Old Law to the Israelites from Mount Sinai.

The discourse begins with the Eight Beatitudes, which are as essential to the Christian way of life as the Ten Commandments have been for the Jewish way of life:

How happy are the poor in spirit;
theirs is the kingdom of heaven.
Happy the gentle:
they shall have the earth for their heritage.
Happy those who mourn:
they shall be comforted.
Happy those who hunger and thirst for what is right:
they shall be satisfied.
Happy the merciful:
they shall have mercy shown them.
Happy the pure in heart:

21

they shall see God.
Happy the peacemakers:
they shall be called children of God.
Happy those who are persecuted in the cause of right:
theirs is the kingdom of heaven. (Matthew 5:3-10 JB)

Looked at closely, these are very paradoxical "commandments."
They do not tell Christians what to do; they tell them what they
will be like if they are living in the kingdom: They will be poor
in spirit, pure in heart, merciful and gentle peacemakers; they
will also thirst for what is right and be persecuted because of it,
and so they will mourn. Not a very happy prospect! And yet
the beatitudes call discipleship a happy life. Why? Because when
disciples live in right relationship with God and one another,
they are comforted, their hunger is satisfied, they are shown
mercy, and they see God; and so they are called God's children,
they live under God's reign, and all the earth is theirs!

The Beatitudes are just as concerned about a new way of
relating between people as the Decalogue was in the early days
of Israel. The commandments spoke of showing honor to God
and to one's parents, and not killing, lying, stealing, cheating
or being jealous. The Beatitudes speak of further qualities which
go beyond the Old Law just as the commandments went beyond
the condition of having no law at all. The Beatitudes add
something really new to revelation, which is a life-style based
on vulnerability, self-emptying and cooperation instead of
merely obeying rules.

Yet if we ask most Christians what it means to be moral,
they think of the commandments. They still think in terms of
Old Testament morality, not New Testament morality. But to
follow Jesus is to follow him out of the old legality of living in
this world's systems and into the new reality of living in a much
larger truth. It is to move beyond the first levels of faith and on
to the mature level. It is to get out of membership and into
discipleship. It is to get past relating to God as lawgiver to
discovering God as lifegiver.

Thus time and again in this sermon on living in the
kingdom, Jesus says in effect, "You have heard that you should
act a certain way in the past. Now I'm not denying that, but I'm

asking you to go even further than that. I'm inviting you to join me where I am, in a whole new way of relating. You have been told not to kill; I'm saying you shouldn't even get needlessly angry. You were told never to break your oath; I'm saying you should be so honest that you never have to swear an oath. You were told to love your neighbors; I'm telling you to love even your enemies" (see Matthew 5:17-48).

Above all, Jesus invites his disciples to follow him into a whole new way of relating to God. He invites them to call God *Abba*, Father, just as he does. He teaches them to pray for the coming of the kingdom in its fullness, when everyone will trust in God enough to give up control and be content with what God gives them day by day. And Jesus challenges them to be so forgiving that they can ask to be forgiven in the same way. The Lord's Prayer, as it has come to be known, is therefore also the disciple's prayer, for it expresses what every true disciple longs for and lives for (see Matthew 6:7-13). Moreover, it is written in the plural for it presumes that disciples live in community.

The way of discipleship is one of happiness and freedom, for those who live in the kingdom are blessed with their hearts' deepest desires, and so they are freed from desiring what everybody else wants. Jesus tells his followers not to worry about money, food and clothing, and not to bother about what other people say or do.

For all its attractiveness, however, the way that Jesus teaches is not easy to find. It can be reached only through conversion, through a total turnabout of thinking, feeling and behaving. It is a moral and cultural about-face! Most people choose the easy path and go the way that everyone else is going, but Jesus says:

> You have to enter the kingdom through the narrow
> gate. The wide gate leads to death, but the road to it
> is smooth, so many people take it. It's a rough road
> to the narrow gate which leads to life. Not many
> people find it. (Matthew 7:13-14)

Those who do find the narrow gate, however, are not meant to live alone in the kingdom. In Matthew's view the

Church is a network of disciples who have accepted Jesus as their Lord and teacher and who join together to learn from Jesus and put his teachings into practice. Nevertheless, the kingdom and the Church are not the same. There are those in the Church who have not yet entered the kingdom; and there are those in the kingdom who are not in the Church.

A perfect example of this is where people stand on the Lordship of Christ. Many Catholics have gone through 12 years of religious education and have never surrendered to Jesus as their personal Lord. They may never have even heard the Lordship of Jesus Christ proclaimed except as a string of words among so many other strings of words at Sunday Mass; they may have no idea that it ought to mean something to them personally. Maybe they associate it with the idea that the Son is a member of the Trinity that rules over the universe in some far off and abstract fashion. But the gospels make clear that those who are in the kingdom accept Jesus as the Lord of their lives and the Lord over all the systems, institutions, nations and cultures of this world (including America and the Catholic Church).

There are many non-Catholics, on the other hand, who understand clearly the Lordship of Christ. It means that either he's first in your life or he's not. Family cannot be first. Career cannot be first. Money cannot be first. Military might cannot be first. And it's not enough just to say, "Jesus is Lord," as though reciting a creed or giving a catechism answer. Lip service does not count. As Jesus himself says:

> It is not anyone who says to me, "Lord, Lord," who
> will enter the kingdom of Heaven, but the person
> who does the will of my Father in heaven.
> (Matthew 7:21 NJB)

What counts is listening to Jesus and letting him teach you how to live. What counts is becoming his personal *disciple*—a word which originally meant "pupil" or "learner." What counts is doing what Jesus teaches, both through the scriptures and through personal contact in prayer. And what Jesus teaches is always the will of the Father.

There are many who follow the teachings of Jesus and do the will of God, even though they are not members of the Church.

The Kingdom and the Church

If we look now at chapters 13 to 18 of this gospel, we find a long section on the kingdom and the Church. Looking at some of these scenes can help us understand what it means to live in the kingdom and what it means to be a member of the Church.

Chapter 13 contains seven different parables on the kingdom of heaven. In the first parable Jesus says that the word of God is like a seed which is sown in the hearts of many, but only those who let it grow within them belong to God's kingdom (Matthew 13:4-9). In the second, he says that those in the kingdom live side by side with everyone else, and you can't always tell who is in it and who is not, although God knows the difference (Matthew 13:24-30). From these parables it is clear that the kingdom is a spiritual reality and not an organized institution.

Still the kingdom is not just in one person; it spreads and grows from person to person. It invades and influences groups and societies. In the third and fourth parables, Jesus says that the kingdom is like a tree that spreads its branches and like yeast that filters through dough, always pervading and organically forming and transforming structures (Matthew 13:31-33). The kingdom is something that touches, inspires and enlivens all things from their very center outward—and changes them.

The next two parables are the shortest, but they are two of my favorites. They show that people can recognize the kingdom when they find it, and when they find it they are willing to give up a great deal to become part of it:

> The kingdom of heaven is like treasure hidden in a field which someone has found; he keeps it safe, goes off happy, sells everything he owns, and buys the field.
>
> Again, the kingdom of heaven is like a merchant looking for fine pearls; when he finds one of great

value he goes and sells everything he owns and buys
it. (Matthew 13:44-46)

I can think of many contemporary examples of how
people have risked security to share life and seek the kingdom:
prayer groups, peace and justice ministries, social agencies,
shelter homes, mission groups, active and contemplative
communities. To join the community of New Jerusalam, in
Cincinnati, for example, individuals have come from all over the
United States, bringing with them only what they could carry
in their suitcases; and families have sold their fine homes in the
suburbs, exchanging them for a richer life in a poorer
neighborhood. If you ask them why they did it, they tell you it
is because they found something in New Jerusalem which was
worth giving up a lot for. In biblical terms, they found a pearl
and knew it was worth the price. Living in the kingdom may
be spiritual, but it is also very real, and it is very attractive when
you discover it.

In the last of the seven parables, Jesus reiterates the idea
that the kingdom is a spiritual reality and, therefore, you may
not know until the end who was in it and who wasn't (Matthew
13:47-50). No prayer group and no parish is perfect. New
Jerusalem isn't perfect. We're weak, sinful people always falling
out of kingdom values and then having to undergo a new
conversion to rediscover them. Sometimes people come to our
community for the wrong reasons, are unopen to conversion,
and never get to know the life of the kingdom. Sometimes people
belong to a parish just because it's convenient. Membership in
the Church doesn't automatically give you citizenship in the
kingdom. To turn toward the kingdom you must turn away from
self. To say, "Thy kingdom come," you must in the next breath
say, "My kingdom go."

In chapter 14 Matthew gives us another image of what it
means to live in the kingdom. It begins with a scene of Jesus in
prayer, communicating with the Father, and getting in touch
with the power of those who live under the reign of God.

Then he made the disciples get into their boat and go
on ahead to the other side of the lake, while he stayed

to send the people home. After the crowd had gone away, he went up the hillside by himself to pray. As night fell, he was there alone. (Matthew 14:22-23)

People who are very action-oriented might wonder why Jesus does this. Often in the gospels we see him going off by himself to pray. They might even object at this point because it looks like he is sending away people who need him, and then going off to spend a good part of the day and night on his own. People like that do not realize, however, that the power to live in the kingdom, and the power to extend the kingdom to others, comes from union with God. If you are not constantly renewing your contact with God, receiving energy from God, you can't do anything. That is, you can't do any more than anybody else can. But if you are in touch with the Father through prayer, you can work miracles.

This is what Matthew shows next. The apostles are out on the lake by themselves and, without the Lord, they start having a rough time of it:

Far out on the lake, the boat was being tossed about on the waves and beaten by strong head winds. Then, just about dawn, Jesus came walking toward them across the lake. (Matthew 14:24-25)

The disciples are those who are learning to live in the kingdom. The boat, we can say, is the external structure around them, their community, the Church. But without Jesus in their midst, the boat is being tossed about. Sometimes the Church seems like it's falling apart, ready to sink. People try all sorts of schemes to bail it out, all kinds of programs and strategies to make it float. They're desperate. But where is the power to stay on top of things? Jesus knows where it is, and so in the midst of the storm he comes walking along to meet them.

At first, they can't believe their eyes:

When the disciples saw him walking on the water, they screamed in terror because they thought it was a ghost. (Matthew 14:26)

One thing that Matthew is trying to get across here is the way Jesus is present to the Church after the resurrection. It's a spiritual presence, but it's also a real presence. Sometimes when we're desperate, when things are falling apart without the Lord, he makes his presence felt, but we are not really sure it's him. It's like he's there, but he's not. We need the eyes of faith to see him. We need some reassurance from the Lord that he is really with us.

> So right away Jesus assured them, "It's all right! Don't worry, it's me!" (Matthew 14:27)

Many times in the scriptures, when God appears to people, he announces his presence by saying, "I am with you. Do not doubt. Do not be afraid." Once we recognize the Lord is with us, we realize that we have nothing to fear.

Faith and fear are polar opposites. They are the bases of two different ways of living. Most of the time most people act on the basis of fear: fear of not making enough money, fear of what others may think, fear of competitors, fear of other countries, even fear of the Church and fear of God's punishment, sad to say.

But Jesus shows us what it means to act on the basis of faith. Faith means standing on the power of God, the love of God, the assurance of God. Faith means believing the good news that the Lord is with us, and that means it is possible to do the impossible. When we become convinced of this, we are ready to step out in faith:

> Then Peter called out, "If it is really you, Lord, tell me to come out to you there on the water." And Jesus said, "Come!" So Peter got out of the boat and started walking across the water toward him.
> (Matthew 14:28-29)

All Jesus says is one word: *Come.* That's the call of a lifetime, the invitation to a whole new way of life. Peter could have asked how, since he could see that there wasn't anything there to hold him up. But he didn't. As a person of faith, that one word from the Lord was all he needed. He expected the unexpected. He couldn't do the impossible on his own, so he did the only thing that was possible: He kept his eyes on the Lord. And as long as he did that, he did the impossible, at least for a while:

> But when Peter looked at the wind making waves, he got frightened and began to sink. "Lord, save me!" he shouted. Right away, Jesus reached out and grabbed him. "What little faith you have!" he exclaimed. "Why did you hesitate?" And as they got into the boat, the wind died down.
> (Matthew 14:30-32)

Whenever we take our eyes off the Lord, the impossible becomes impossible again. We no longer expect the unexpected. We start to fear what everybody else fears. We begin to sink, and we know it. We start drowning in our own confusion, worrying about the dangers we see. And that's when we resort to the most often used prayer in the world: "Lord, help me!"

But all Jesus asks for is faith. He asks only that we keep our eyes on him and trust him. Then, if we take the Lord's hand, we can get up and walk on the water again. Like Peter, we can see that we're all wet if we try to make it on our own. Like Peter, too, we might even feel a little foolish about our lack of faith. But at times like that, if we're fortunate enough to have experiences like that and learn from them, we learn the real meaning of faith. We learn who is the Lord, and why he is the Lord. We are ready to let him sustain us, not just when we're in trouble, but all the time. We are ready to let him be our Lord. We are no longer our own.

Matthew's portrayal of this readiness to confess the Lordship of Christ comes a few scenes later in chapter 16. Jesus is with his disciples again, this time near the town of Caesaria Philippi, and he asks them what people are thinking about him. The disciples answer that many think he might be John the Baptist or one of the earlier prophets come back to life. But then he turns to them and asks, "But you, who do you say I am?" (Matthew 16:15).

29

This is the rock bottom question that every person has to answer if they call themselves Christians. This is really getting down to the basics. There is nothing more fundamental in the Christian life than asking, "Who do I say Jesus is?" And if you really ask yourself that unavoidable question, and face the issue head on, you know you can't get the answer out of a book. It has to be something that comes from your heart. It has to be an answer that is based on your own experience of Jesus. It has to come out of your own life, if it is to be true at all.

Of all the disciples, the one who really learned the lesson of faith that morning out on the lake was Peter. And so before any of the others can respond, Peter speaks up: "You are the Christ, the Son of the living God!" (Matthew 16:16). He confesses immediately that Jesus is the messiah, the anointed one of God. Jesus is the one that all of Israel had been hoping for, a savior sent by God. And how does Peter know this? Not because he read it in a book. How can he be so sure about it? Not because he deduced it in his mind. The answer comes from deep within him. So Jesus tells him:

> You are a happy man, Simon son of John! Nothing on earth could have told you that. My heavenly Father revealed it to you. Because of that, I'd say you're a rock, as your name Peter says. (Matthew 16:17-18)

Simon's nickname meant something like "Rocky" in Greek, but traditional translations have kept the original spelling, Peter. So Jesus here is telling Peter he's as solid as his name. He has really reached the rock-bottom answer to the question Jesus put to him, and which he puts to every one of us as well. He has reached that fundamental trust of the true disciple, the true learner. Trust, or faith, is the foundation of every natural and every supernatural relationship. And if Peter and the other disciples could reach that deep level of trust in Jesus and faith in the Father, the work of building the Church could go on. Thus Jesus continues:

> That's the rock that I will build my church on. Nothing will be able to stand in its way, not even the gates of

hell. I will give you the keys of the kingdom of heaven.
(Matthew 16:18-19)

Jesus is saying that on faith like that he can build a community; on that kind of foundation he can establish his Church. If people can trust one another at a very deep level, if they have faith in Jesus as their Lord and are willing to learn from him how to accept the gift of faith from the Father, then the Church can start building and growing.

Notice that although the foundation of the Church is as solid as a rock, the Church itself is expanding, growing. Jesus speaks of the Church as a movement, as a dynamic force which nothing can prevail against. Wherever the Church meets resistance, whether it be hardness of heart or even satanic opposition, it will not be stopped. For Jesus will give it the keys to unlock every door, the keys of undying faith and self-giving love, which can ultimately break through any resistance. And through those open doors, the good news of the kingdom can be heard by every human heart and proclaimed in every human society.

The mission of the Church is thus the same as the mission of Jesus: to preach the good news that the kingdom is here, that it has already arrived in part, and that it is spreading to all those who will open their hearts to it. But the mission of the Church is also to preach the Lordship of Christ, who is Lord of the kingdom as well as head of the Church. It is by being a community of Jesus' disciples, of people who have trusted him enough to learn his way of loving one another and the Father, that the kingdom of God will be established on earth.

The establishment of God's kingdom in its fullness is the goal of the Church. The Church is only a means to the end which is the kingdom. For the kingdom is a radical relationship of love and trust with a loving and faithful God. From that, everything else follows, including the radical relationship of love and trust we have with one another. And it all happens under the Lordship of Christ, for we are his disciples.

All too often in our history, however, we have behaved as though the Church were not the means but the end itself. We have preached the Church instead of preaching the kingdom

31

and the Lordship of Christ. Yet Jesus wasted no time in preaching Israel. He loved Israel and he saw it as his Father's means for bringing the kingdom into the world. So he did not fight Israel or Judaism, but he constantly called them back to the purpose for which God had chosen the Israelites and given them the Jewish Law.

We ought to have the same attitude toward the Church and Catholicism. If we are truly disciples of Jesus, we should not proclaim the Church or exalt Catholicism. That misses the whole point of what Jesus was about. Worse than that, instead of furthering the kingdom, it subverts the kingdom. For it hides the good news of God's reign behind religious works and institutional walls which, to many people, look like so much bad news. It breaks the First Commandment and makes an idol of the Church.

Matthew's vision of the breaking out of the kingdom into the world grows richer and broader from this point onward in his gospel. In chapter 17 Jesus is transfigured before the disciples, giving them a glimpse of the gloriousness of the kingdom in his own glory. In chapter 18 Jesus teaches his disciples how to love, serve and forgive each other in the Church. In chapter 21 Jesus is proclaimed as the messiah by the people in his triumphal ride into Jerusalem.

The Fullness of God's Reign
But then the stage darkens as we view the scenes of Jesus' arrest and trial and crucifixion. The way into the kingdom is a rough road, and the gate to it is narrow, just as Jesus had said earlier. The way of Jesus is not always an easy one, for the way of self-giving love is often one of suffering. The day is sometimes darkest just before the dawn. But the dawn arrives, just as Jesus had said it would, on the day of resurrection. And so he enters into the fullness of his glory, the fullness of his Father's kingdom.

In chapter 28, the last chapter of this gospel, the risen Jesus appears to his disciples. They are now his Church, and he is now their Lord. He reminds them of their purpose, which is to open the kingdom to the whole world through the mission of the Church:

I have been given all authority in heaven and earth. Go, therefore, and make the people of all nations my disciples. Immerse them in the reality of the Father and the Son and the Holy Spirit. Teach them to do everything that I told you to do. And remember, I am with you always, even to the end of time.

(Matthew 28:18-20)

CHAPTER TWO

Mark and John's Good News: Jesus Is Lord!

Mark and John were two evangelists whose encounters with Christ led them to present very different pictures of the Lord. Mark's gospel is the earliest of the four that we find in the New Testament, probably written around 65 to 70 A.D. The Gospel According to John is the latest, probably written toward the end of the first century. Modern scholarship suggests that neither of these writers met Jesus before his resurrection, yet each in his own way understands what it means to be a disciple of Christ.

Even though the two gospels present very different theologies of Christ, both were written in Christian communities and both were accepted in the early Church. The Church did not say that because they were different, one had to be right and the other had to be wrong. Each gospel in its own way expressed the mystery of Christ and led others to experience the risen Lord. Both gospels grew out of the first disciples' relationship with Jesus and led new Christians to understand more fully the Lordship of Christ. The Church was pluralistic and had room for differing emphases from the very beginning.

Mark's Challenge: To Enter the Mystery of Suffering

The writer Mark is most likely the same John Mark who is mentioned by Luke in the Acts of the Apostles and by Paul in some of the epistles. Other early Christian writers say that this gospel was written in Rome, and that the evangelist had heard the preaching of Peter as well. At any rate, the gospel writer gives us a picture of Jesus which is very close to the preaching of the apostles, but which is presented with a very definite intention.

Mark probably wrote shortly after the great persecution in Rome (64 A.D.) in which both Peter and Paul were martyred. Up till then, the gentile converts in Rome had experienced only the *glory* of Christ. They had accepted Jesus as their savior; they had experienced miraculous healings of body and spirit at the hands of the apostles; and they had witnessed the wonderful growth of the Christian community. They did not fully realize, however, that the call to discipleship meant accepting not only the glory of Christ but also his suffering.

Mark's audience had to enter into the mystery of suffering as Jesus had done and as the Roman martyrs had done. The purpose of Mark's gospel was therefore to remind Christians who acknowledged Jesus as the messiah that he is also the suffering servant. It instructs them that Jesus' way of salvation is a way through darkness and death.

Understanding Mark's intention helps explain what is sometimes called the "messianic secret." At the very beginning of his gospel, Mark announces that he is proclaiming the good news about Jesus Christ, the messiah, the Son of God (Mark 1:1). But in the first half of the gospel no one realizes this except wicked spirits, whom Jesus warns not to reveal who he is (Mark 1:34; 3:11-12). When Peter and the Twelve recognize that he is the messiah in the eighth chapter, again Jesus admonishes them not to tell anyone (Mark 8:27-30). All through the second half of the gospel none of the disciples understands that the messiah must suffer and die, even when he tries to tell them (Mark 8:31-33; 9:30-31; 10:32-34). When Jesus is finally arrested, they all run away (Mark 14:50-52). It is not until the crucifixion that Jesus is recognized as the Son of God.

All through his gospel, then, Mark is reminding his readers that even though they know who Jesus is, many well-intentioned people do not, and in fact it may only be the wicked of this world who clearly perceive the threat that Jesus poses to them. He is also reminding them that even though they may confess Jesus as the messiah, they may not fully appreciate what that means until, like the Twelve, they confront the mystery of suffering.

The "messianic secret," therefore, is really the difficulty of coming to grips with the Lordship of Jesus and his way of salvation. It is a teaching device which Mark uses to instruct his readers, including us, that the full meaning of Christ is elusive. Mark's Jesus does not want us to proclaim that he is Lord and savior until we fully understand that his way leads to the cross. In other words, don't say "Jesus is Lord" too quickly or too lightly. You need to realize what you are saying and what it implies!

The Mystery of the Messiah Unfolds

Mark begins his gospel with the public life of Jesus. Right after he is baptized in the Jordan and tempted in the wilderness, Jesus goes into Galilee and proclaims:

> The time has come! The reign of God is here! Turn around and believe the good news! (Mark 1:15)

In these three short phrases, Mark both summarizes the initial teaching of Jesus and tells readers what he wants them to do.

First, the time is here. Salvation is now. There is no other time to be saved. It's not in the past, and it's not in the future. It's not when Jesus was born, and it's not when we were baptized. It's not when we will go to confession, and it's not when we will die. It's now or never. Either we are listening to Jesus now, or we're not. Either we are living in the kingdom now, or we're not.

Second, the place is here. Redemption takes place right where we are. We don't have to go to the Holy Land to find it. We don't have to go to Rome or even to church to find it. God's kingdom is wherever we allow God to reign, wherever we put God's truth first. If it's not here, it's not anywhere. And if we do not enter into a personal relationship with the Lord, it is nowhere.

So, third, we have to turn our lives around. We have to repent, undergo conversion, experience a change of heart and mind, turn away from ourselves. We have to positively believe the good news that God loves us no less than he loved Jesus. God cannot save us unless we accept being accepted, which is one of the most difficult surrenders possible.

The next short section shows the calling of the first disciples. When Jesus says, "Follow me," right away they leave their work and their families to join him. They don't even give it a second thought. You can't think your way into the kingdom. You can't deduce the reign of God. You have to meet Jesus "hands on," and respond to him concretely and specifically, just as the first disciples did. Chances are, though, you won't really understand at first what you are getting yourself into, just as the first disciples did not.

Immediately after Jesus called the disciples, he performs a number of miraculous cures. He heals people who are sick, paralyzed and possessed by evil spirits. Sometimes when these texts are taken out of context, they are used to prove that Jesus is God. But at this point in his gospel, Mark is saying something quite different. He is telling us what disciples are called to do. He is showing how the power to heal is available not only to the Son of God but also to all daughters and sons of God. He is showing that Christians are called, like Christ, to care for and cure those who are sick in body and spirit.

And yet, Mark warns us, that is not the whole of it. After some of the cures, Jesus tells the people not to broadcast what he did. This is another variation of the messianic secret. Jesus can work wonders by the power of God, but the messiah is not a religious magician and discipleship is not measured by miracles. Mark is preparing his readers—just as Jesus is preparing his followers—for the revelation that, in the end, discipleship means following Jesus to the cross.

Many of the miraculous cures take place in response to faith. The faith of Jesus reaches out to those who need healing, and when their faith reaches back to him, they are healed. The power of God is released through faith. If we trust in Divine Love, sickness can be cured. If we surrender to the goodness of God, evil can be overcome. But where faith is absent, not much can be done. Mark shows this a little later, at the beginning of chapter 6, when Jesus is not able to work any miracles because the people he reaches out to are closed and fearful.

We might expect these miraculous cures to make Jesus popular. Of course the people he heals are happy but, ironically, his works of mercy lead the local authorities to suspect him of evil. No doubt this was actually true in Jesus' life, but Mark makes sure to mention it because the same thing had happened to the Christians in Rome. The apostles performed miracles, people who joined the community were healed, and yet the Roman authorities persecuted them.

Doing the Father's work sometimes leads to conflict. Helping the poor can be seen as a threat by the rich. Telling people to love their enemies can be seen as a danger to national security. Giving food to the hungry can be seen as undercutting the economy. Performing miracles of healing through the power of God can be seen as a threat to cherished beliefs that such things just can't happen.

Those whose eyes are closed by moral blindness cannot recognize the work of God for what it really is. But those close to Jesus can also fail to realize who he is and what the nature of his mission is. Even though the people of Galilee are eager to see this new wonder-worker, his relatives take quite a different view of him:

> He returned to the house where he was staying, but
> such a large crowd of people gathered there that he
> and his disciples could not even eat. When his family
> heard what was going on, they wanted to force him
> to go home with them, for they thought he was out
> of his mind. (Mark 4:20-21)

Our image of what Jesus looked like to his own contemporaries is more influenced by Christian art and pious sentiment than by gospel scenes like this one. Hollywood movies show us a beautiful Caucasian Jesus, dressed in a snow white robe, hair perfectly styled—obviously God! Yet here we see an ordinary Jewish Jesus, doing such extraordinary things that the people closest to him think he's gone crazy!

Mark wrote his gospel much closer to the time of Jesus than the other evangelists, so one suspects that scenes like this are also closer to the facts. And when we reflect on it, it is clear that Jesus was not understood by the people of his day for, in the end, they executed him. Jesus was not concerned with appearances but with a deeper reality. He was not worried about how he looked to other people; he cared only about being true to his Father and speaking that truth to the world, whether or not the world wanted to hear it.

But there was one group which Jesus hoped would understand him, and that was his disciples. In the chapters that follow, Jesus teaches them plainly and in parables. He continues to preach repentance and to heal, and then he sends the disciples off to do likewise. By word and deed he is teaching them what it means to be Godlike. Then finally he makes the breakthrough. He asks his disciples who they think he really is, and Peter answers for them all when he says, "You are the Christ" (Mark 8:29). This is the first climax of Mark's Gospel.

As we have already seen in Matthew, Jesus' question is addressed not only to the Twelve but also to all readers of the gospel. Mark is as concerned as any modern-day evangelist that people appreciate not only who Jesus was but who he is for them. Anyone who has heard Jesus asking them that existential question, "Who do you say I am?," knows that answering it out of conviction becomes a decisive factor in life. Acknowledging Jesus not just as the Lord but as *my* Lord, not just as the savior but as *my* savior demands a personal conversion. It is a revolutionary turning point in any person's life. Here, in Mark's gospel, it is also a major turning point.

The Mystery of the Suffering Messiah

From this point onward, Jesus openly admits that he is the messiah. He calls himself "the son of man," a messianic title from the Old Testament Book of Daniel. He no longer tells the spirits he casts out or the people he cures to be silent about him. His disciples now understand who he is.

But they do not yet understand *what* he is. They have

their own ideas of what a messiah ought to be. They do not yet realize that the salvation Christ will bring is not an easy victory. They have not yet connected Jesus with the figure of the suffering servant in the Book of Isaiah.

Mark is concerned that his own community understand this connection. It took the Twelve a long time to comprehend it, and so Mark repeats the point three times. Each time, Jesus tells the disciples that the messiah must suffer and die. Each time, Jesus tries to teach them that the salvation he brings comes only through self-sacrifice. And, each time, they miss the point.

Immediately after Peter admits that Jesus is the messiah, Jesus tries to tell them what this really means:

> He began to teach them what the son of man would have to undergo: rejection by his own religious leaders, execution, and three days later, resurrection. He did not try to hide anything from them. But Peter took him on the side and told him not to say things like that. Then Jesus turned around and, eyeing the disciples, reprimanded Peter: "Get out of my sight, you tempter! You're looking at things from a human point of view, not God's." (Mark 8:31-33)

Somehow Peter is always first. He is the first to follow Jesus. He is the first to recognize him as the Christ. He is also the first to disbelieve, to misunderstand, to lie and to betray. He thinks of success the way most people do, in terms of glory. But Jesus tells Peter and the disciples that the way to succeed in the kingdom is through self-denial:

> Anyone who wants to be a follower of mine has to put himself aside, shoulder his cross, and go the way that I go. Whoever holds on to his own life will lose it. But whoever lets go of his life for the sake of me and the good news will redeem it. (Mark 8:34-35)

Jesus is trying to lead them to a deeper level of living, a deeper wisdom and a deeper faith. He is revealing the secret of suffering servanthood, the way of trusting surrender to the Father. A short while later, he takes the disciples aside and again tells them what this will mean for him:

> The son of man is going to be delivered into the hands of people who will put him to death. But three days after he is killed, he will rise. (Mark 9:31)

Mark says right after this that the disciples do not understand what Jesus is saying, but they are afraid to question him about it. We ourselves are the same way. Jesus tells us plainly in the gospels what he is up to. But we are afraid to ask what this might imply for our own lives. It's too risky. Perhaps we understand it vaguely, and we do not want to face the implications of understanding it too clearly. It seems that it is just as hard to believe in resurrection as it is to accept crucifixion.

The Paschal Mystery

In theological language, Jesus is talking about what is often called "the paschal mystery." We hear those words but, like the first disciples, we do not question what they mean. It is safer to think that they refer to something really religious and remote. But Jesus is simply talking about life, his and ours. He is saying that the way to his unique kind of life is by giving up our usual kind of life. The paschal mystery is the experience of entering into new life through death.

Yet we have to admit that Jesus' way to life is paradoxical, by human standards. That's one reason why it's hard to understand. The way Jesus leads is not the way we usually want to go. Mark brings this out so clearly in the very next scene:

> They went on to Capernaum, and when they arrived at the house where they were staying, Jesus asked, "What were all of you discussing back there on the road?" But they did not want to say anything, since they had been arguing about which of them was the most important. So he sat down, called the twelve around him, and explained, "Anyone who wants to be the most important has to be the least

important—the servant of all the others."
(Mark 9:33-35)

Like the Twelve, we usually want to be on top, but Jesus calls us to be happy at the bottom. We want to be the boss, but he wants us to be the servant. We want to be grown-up and admired, but he tells us to be like children. We want to achieve a lot, but he says we need to receive a lot:

Truly, anyone who does not accept the kingdom of God like a child will never enter it. (Mark 10:15)

That looks like giving up a lot, so Mark inserts the story of the rich young man at this point. He is a good person, he keeps all the commandments; but when Jesus invites him to give up his wealth for the sake of the kingdom, he cannot bring himself to do it. So Jesus points out to his followers how wealth easily prevents people from experiencing the riches of the kingdom. Sometimes religion itself becomes a possession instead of a way of self-surrender. Jesus therefore invites him to this surrender. Unfortunately, the young man turns away. Too often the rich, the religious, and the self-sufficient know nothing about self-surrender. Jesus says that is a dangerous way to live:

It is easier for a camel to pass through the eye of a needle than for a wealthy person to enter the kingdom of God. (Mark 10:25)

The way into life is along the rough road and through the narrow gate. Jesus tries again to tell the disciples what this will mean for him:

Now we are heading for Jerusalem, and the son of man is going to be put in the hands of the Jewish leaders. They will condemn him to death and hand him over to the Romans, who will mock him and spit at him and flog him and kill him. But three days later, he will rise. (Mark 10:33-34)

You'd think by now the disciples would be starting to get the message. But no, they're dense. They're just as dense as all the Christians who hear about the paschal mystery and never really understand what it means. The disciples do not see, and so James and John naively ask the Lord if he will do them a favor. They ask if they can sit in glory at his side when he establishes the messianic kingdom (Mark 10:35-37).

You can almost hear the sigh from the depths of Jesus' heart when he hears their request. How agonizing it must have been for him to keep patiently loving these 12 ignorant men! They had no sense of the spiritual reality he was referring to, no awareness of the kingdom he was proclaiming. And so he turns to them and says:

> You do not know what you are asking for. Can you drink the cup that I will drink, or be immersed in the same bath that I will be immersed in? (Mark 10:38)

Jesus is trying to bring them back to reality, to his reality as the suffering servant. He is referring to the cup of pain he will have to swallow, the bath of anguish he will be drowned in. He is alluding to the suffering which is the only way into the kingdom of his Father.

The other disciples get indignant when they hear what James and John are asking. Once again Jesus has to sit them down and explain to them:

> You know how the so-called rulers of nations like to set themselves over other people? And how those at the top like to make their authority felt? Well, with you it has to be different. If you want to be important, serve others. And if you want to be at the top, then slave to help everyone else. The son of man himself did not come to be served but to serve, to give his life so that everyone might be set free. (Mark 10:42-45)

If only the Church had shared Jesus' bias toward the bottom the past 2,000 years! If only we had seriously believed him, how much sooner we would have seen the coming of the kingdom! If only we had truly listened to the gospels, how differently Western history would have unfolded! Instead we have made easy friends with power, prestige and possession—even in the name of God and the Church.

We use the name of Christ and have fine theological terms for what we do, but often what we do is no different from what everyone else does. We run our dioceses and parishes the same way that governments and businesses are run. We ask what fund-raisers will save our schools, what strategies will rescue our religion programs, what speakers will draw the largest crowds to fill our empty auditoriums. Although we pray to God for help, we act as though good planning and hard work, theological reason, efficiency and organization will save the Church.

But only the way of suffering service will save the Church. Only the way of faith will build a faith community. There is no easy way to do it. There is no worldly way to do it. There is no other way to build a faith community except by self-surrender and allowing the little ones to influence our lives. The only way is to make Jesus our Lord and suffer with him in solidarity with others.

Many Catholics have never known the kingdom which is the heart and soul of the Church. They have never been part of a network of believers which is built on kingdom values. They have only belonged, attended, or contributed but never really lived in a new way. Their life is not really an alternative to living in the world.

The kingdom comes when right relationships come into being. It comes, first, when there are people who have a personal relationship with Jesus Christ, developed through time spent in personal prayer every day. It comes when there are people who have heard the call of Christ to become his disciples, and who have devoted hours to reading his word in the scriptures, responding to his word in their hearts, learning what he wants to teach them. It comes only after years of learning from the Lord what it means to follow him, what it means to live the paschal mystery.

The kingdom comes, second, when there are people who have a personal relationship with one another. They are not playing roles. They are not playing teacher and student, pastor and parishioner, cleric and layperson. They are just being Linda and Harry and Frank and Sue. They are being real with one another, laughing and crying with each other, helping each other out and sharing one another's burdens. They are being honest with one another, sharing their questions and doubts, as well as what they've learned from their experiences with others and from listening to the Lord.

The kingdom never comes in fullness, but sometimes it does come in power and glory at those times of celebration with others who are living under the reign of God. Sometimes, too, it comes in moments of intense togetherness, when people reach out to others to give help or ask for help, and when they overcome their differences and experience forgiveness. In our community of New Jerusalem we have seen so many people strengthened and healed in moments like that, when we know the Lord is present in our midst, working among us, enabling us to live in the Spirit.

At times like that, when we are united as a single body under the headship of Christ, we know from our own experience what it means to be a Church. We come in contact with the heart and soul of the larger Church to which we all belong. We know full well that the Church is not the kingdom, but the Church is where the kingdom comes alive, whenever it does come. And we have also seen that wherever and whenever the kingdom comes, the Church comes alive.

The Journey to Jerusalem

In Mark's gospel, from the moment the disciples recognize that Jesus is the messiah, he heads them toward Jerusalem teaching them all the things we have just been discussing. He is leading them on a journey of faith explaining to them what it means to accept his Lordship and to trust completely in the Father. He is heading toward his destiny and he is bringing the disciples with him, building them into a community of faith as they walk together on that journey.

Our experience at New Jerusalem has been a lot like that. We started as a bunch of young people, still wet behind the ears after our baptism in the Spirit, following the Lord where he was leading us, learning that to be his disciples meant suffering with and for each other. It was not all fun by any means, but there have been some moments of glory, some moments of transfiguration, when we were really glad that we had left everything to follow him. And slowly, in retrospect, we discovered that our greatest resurrections always came after our greatest crucifixions, both as individuals and as a community.

In Mark's gospel Jesus leads his first disciples to his final crucifixion. He has already experienced minor crucifixions in being attacked by the Jewish leaders, in being rejected by some of those who heard him, in being misunderstood by those who were close to him. But now he moves even further into that space of loneliness and alienation, that place where he must stand on the love of the Father, and trust in him alone.

By depicting Jesus as heading resolutely into that space while bringing the disciples along with him, Mark is showing his own community that they too must allow themselves to be led into suffering. Every scene of the passion is a lesson showing how the master suffered, teaching that suffering is inevitable for the true disciple.

In chapter 15 Jesus is more alone than he has ever been. Every human prop has been removed. There is no reason why he should continue to believe that he is the Father's beloved Son. He is being mocked by those around him. All the disciples are gone. Now he stands alone, standing on the remembrance of the Father's love, moving through the darkness in faith.

Inwardly he is being led by the Father, being used by the Father to fulfill his mission. Outwardly he is led by soldiers, abused by men who do not know what they are doing. He is nailed to the cross and lifted up for all to see where obedience to the Father's will inevitably leads.

Now there are no miracles. Now everything is ordinary, just as pain is ordinary. There are no signs from heaven. There is only incarnational faith redeeming the human situation in the midst of a sinful world. There is only the incarnate Word speaking in silence from Calvary.

Those who do not know who and what he is tell him to perform a miracle and save himself if he is really the messiah. But Jesus does not answer them. He is listening to the Father leading him onward still, leading him deeper still. He comes close to despair, but in the end his faith in the Father's love becomes the hope of resurrection. The only way to know that is to surrender in trust to the Father. The only way to gain new life is by giving up the old.

At the moment of his death, Jesus is finally recognized as the one whom Mark announced at the beginning of his gospel. A Roman soldier, a supposed nonbeliever, stands before the cross and confesses, "This man was truly a son of God" (Mark 15:39).

Ironically, it is not the disciples who perceive and proclaim the deepest truth about the Lord. They have seen his miracles, they have heard his teachings, and yet they all have run away from Jesus and his mission. In all probability the Twelve did abandon Jesus at the end; all the gospels indicate as much. But Mark uses this historical fact to teach a hard lesson to his own community which he sees as not really understanding the sonship of Jesus, as having forgotten their mission as disciples to suffer with the Lord.

The only ones who stand with Jesus at the cross are women, the so-called weaker sex. Only they have the strength to be with him in his suffering. Only they have the faith to see it through to the bitter end. Only they are there at the tomb on the third day to discover the beautiful truth of the resurrection and to experience the Lord in his glory. To the weak ones of the world the power of the kingdom is revealed, and through them the good news of Jesus' Lordship is first announced.

Mark's gospel does not end with condemnation, however, but with forgiveness. Although the disciples abandoned Jesus, he does not abandon them. He appears to them and, after chiding them for their lack of faith, he passes on to them his mission to proclaim the good news of the kingdom. Anyone who accepts the reign of God can enter it; and anyone who accepts it totally, like Jesus, will experience its beginnings even in this life.

Mark thus bequeaths to his community the message that the risen Lord has not and will not abandon them. His victorious presence as the conquered conqueror remains with them. But his presence is perceived only by those who believe even unto

death, until everything else is taken away.
Then only he remains.

John's Challenge: To Understand the Lordship of Jesus

There could be no greater contrast than between the gospels of
Mark and John. Mark's is the earliest, John's is the last (written
around 90-100 A.D.), and a generation of meditation on the life
and message of Jesus lies between them. Yet John's purpose is
similar to Mark's, as he states clearly toward the close of his
gospel:

> These things have been recorded so that you might
> believe that Jesus is the messiah, the Son of God, and
> so that through this faith you might find the life which
> bears his name. (John 20:31)

Like Mark, John preaches the Lordship of Jesus and his
divine sonship. His is concerned with the reader making a
personal act of faith in Jesus and, through that, entering into
divine life as sons and daughters of the Father. The evangelist
does not want to preserve the words and deeds of Jesus exactly
as they happened for the sake of future history. He wants instead
to communicate the relationship which he himself has with the
Lord, and from which he draws his life.

John does this through a series of finely crafted literary
dialogues interspersed with stories which are only sometimes
similar to those found in the other three gospels. In all likelihood
these dialogues are the result of the author's encounters with
the risen Jesus in prayer rather than the product of his memory
of what Jesus actually said in his lifetime.

In John's gospel Jesus' words are often quite poetic and
philosophical. Jesus speaks less like a carpenter from Nazareth
and more like an educated Jew raised in the Hellenistic world.
For this reason it seems unlikely that this written gospel came
from the hand of the John who was one of the Twelve. The
"disciple that Jesus loved" was not a Hellenistic philosopher but
a Galilean fisherman. (It is much more likely that this John wrote

the book of Revelation, which has a very different, very Jewish, style.) According to some ancient traditions, however, the disciple John gathered around himself a community in Ephesus, near Greece. Most probably he is the authority behind this gospel, even if the final author in the modern sense may have been one of his disciples. It was still the school and influence of John the beloved disciple which formed the outlook of the final composer of the gospel.

The Book of Signs: Signals of Lordship

John's gospel is unique in that, unlike any of the other gospels, it begins with a beautiful prologue:

> In the beginning was the Word:
> the Word was with God
> and the Word was God.
> He was with God in the beginning.
> Through him all things came into being,
> not one thing had its being except through him.
> What has come into being in him was life,
> life that was the light of men;
> and light shines in darkness,
> and darkness could not overpower it. (John 1:1-5 NJB)

This prologue, which goes on for 18 verses, may be a hymn which John's community sang at their liturgical celebrations. It is a theological poem which summarizes their understanding of the Lordship of Jesus: He is the Word which God has spoken in the world; he is God become flesh; he is the Father's only Son; he is divine light and love made incarnate.

At the beginning of the prologue, John speaks about the Word of God being present at the creation of the world; John then symbolically gives us a new creation in seven days. The Word-become-flesh now creates a new people who are not of the world but of the Spirit, and in the opening week of Jesus' ministry he gathers a community around himself, calling the first disciples to faith in him and in the Father.

John's gospel is filled with symbolism which expresses the evangelist's profound understanding of the events he is describing, and which are meant to lead the reader to that same deep understanding through prayer and service. This is another of the reasons why John is the most theological and least historical of the four gospels in many places.

On the first day of the new creation, for example, we are introduced to John the Baptist; on the second day he sees Jesus walking toward him and says, "Look, there is the lamb of God who takes away the sin of the world" (John 1:29). In no other gospel does John the Baptist use these words, but the evangelist uses them to introduce two ideas: that Jesus is the suffering servant who is humble as a lamb (Isaiah 53:6-7) and that Jesus is the paschal lamb who is sacrificed so that others can be freed from the slavery of sin (Exodus 12:1-14). Almost every sentence in this gospel contains something symbolic to meditate on.

On the third and fourth days, Jesus meets the first disciples and invites them to follow him. The descriptions are very different from those we find in the other three gospels, and yet it is the very same story, the very same theme of leaving everything in order to enter into a personal relationship with the Lord.

John lets his readers fill the story of the calling of the rest of the Twelve, for by the end of the week they are all with him. Then, on the seventh day, Jesus begins to reveal his glory as the Son of God by performing the first of his miracles.

In this gospel the miraculous works of Jesus are always referred to as "signs," for they are signs of Jesus' mission, signals of his divinity and symbols of the salvation which he brings. Scripture scholars refer to the first 12 chapters of the gospel as the Book of Signs because they contain all the miracle stories. The signs lead some to faith in Jesus while others remain in disbelief. In the second half of the gospel, Jesus no longer performs signs but instructs those who already believe in him about his way of salvation.

Another unique feature of this gospel is the way that it refers to unbelievers as "the Jews." In many places the antagonism between Jesus and the Jews is so great that the gospel appears to be antisemitic, until we recall that Jesus himself and all those who believe in him are Jewish. Who then are these Jews the gospel is talking about?

A careful reading of the text shows that whenever there is animosity between Jesus and the Jews, "the Jews" are always unbelieving Jews. The Jews in John's gospel are therefore symbolic. They symbolize stubborn disbelief. They symbolize the rejection of the Lord. They symbolize the self-righteousness which led to the crucifixion of Jesus and the persecution of the early Christians (all of whom were Jewish!) suffering at the hand of other Jews.

The unbelieving Jews and their leaders, the Pharisees, also symbolize ritualistic religion. For John and his community, the empty formalism of religious institutions stands in sharp contrast with the fullness of life which comes from a personal relationship with Christ. One of the great themes running through this gospel is the difference between religion and relationship, between lifeless religious practices and living with the Lord. And the symbol of dead religion for John is Judaism and anything connected with it.

The Sign of New Wine

We see this right away in the first of Jesus' signs, the miracle at Cana. Everyone has been invited to a wedding—that is, to unity with God. But traditional religion runs dry, and so Mary comes to Jesus saying, "They have no wine" (John 2:3). It is no accident that Jesus calls her "woman," for she calls to mind the woman of Genesis, the woman of the Apocalypse, and the women in the other parts of John's gospel. Woman is the symbol of humanity before God, receptive and responsive to the divine initiative, to bring forth life. Here in this story humanity is turning to Jesus, complaining that religion is empty, it no longer gives meaning to life, it no longer gives joy to existence.

At first Jesus says that it is not yet time for him to do something, but the woman knows that the hour of redemption is at hand. She tells the waiters to do what Jesus says, and in so doing she symbolically tells all those who are waiting for salvation to turn to Jesus and do what he says. We want the wine of life, we want to taste something better than the daily drudgery which the world and cheap religion offer us.

The inability of ritualistic religion to satisfy us is symbolized by the empty water jars used for Jewish purification rituals. But if, like the waiters, we do what Jesus asks, he gives us something to replace what the old religious practices were meant to convey. He gives us wine for water! We thought we had something good, but it turns out to be cheap wine compared with what he offers us. The relationship he invites us into is more than we ever could have expected. It sets our heads spinning! It makes us drunk with gladness! It's like gallons and gallons of the best wine!

Much of John's gospel is directed against cheap religiosity. Well-run churches and sermons that are easy to listen to may appeal to us at first, but they do not really satisfy our deep spiritual hunger. They are empty, and what they seem to hold for us will turn out to be as tasteless as standing water.

The next scene confirms this. Jesus marches into the temple which, for John, is the symbol of the buying and selling of God. Jesus chases out the buyers and sellers of religious peace of mind, disturbing them with the very zeal which drove David and Solomon to build this house for God. When he is asked to justify his act of "civil disobedience," his violent protest action, Jesus answers, "Destroy this temple, and in three days I will raise it up!" (John 2:19). He has moved religion from something centered in buildings to something centered in his own body, his people.

John is referring not only to the resurrection. This gospel was written after the temple in Jerusalem had been destroyed in 70 A.D., and so John is also alluding to the fact that Christian communities are rising up out of the ashes of Judaism. The symbolism in John's gospel is very rich because the symbols, such as those here, have multiple meanings.

Signs in Birth, Wind and Water

Another way that John reveals the deeper message of his gospel is through artfully constructed dialogues. Often someone comes to Jesus to ask a question, but Jesus draws the person into a conversation. As the dialogue goes back and forth, Jesus moves it to a deeper level where he can reveal a meaning that the other person does not fully understand, but which the reader of the gospel is invited to ponder.

In chapter 3, for example, a leader of the Jews named Nicodemus comes to see Jesus secretly at night, since he is afraid of what others might think if they saw them together. After he says a few words, Jesus tells him that a person cannot see the kingdom of God without being "born from above." But what does that mean? Nicodemus complains that an old man cannot be reborn, to which Jesus responds:

> In all truth I tell you,
> no one can enter the kingdom of God
> without being born through water and the Spirit;
> what is born of human nature is human;
> what is born of the Spirit is spirit.
> Do not be surprised when I say:
> You must be born from above. (John 3:5-7 NJB)

Immediately we know that Jesus is not talking about physical rebirth but about spiritual rebirth. He is talking about being renewed in the Spirit, about letting God's spirit lead us instead of being led by the spirit of the world. To explain what he means, Jesus continues:

> The wind blows where it pleases;
> you can hear its sound,
> but you cannot tell where it comes from or where it
>   is going.
> So it is with everyone who is born of the Spirit.
> (John 3:8 NJB)

From the world's point of view, Spirit-led people are unpredictable. And yet in another sense they are completely predictable. They are always trying to do God's will. They are always trying to do what is obviously good, regardless of social conventions, regardless of what other people think. And that is exactly the freedom of the sons and daughters of God. That is the freedom you find in the kingdom. Yet most people do not want to be that free. They are already too settled in their old routines. They are already too comfortable in their own life-styles.

In many ways they are like the woman at the well who speaks to Jesus in the next dialogue. She wants something more from life, so Jesus offers her "living water." Another enigmatic phrase! She asks how he plans to get it out of the well. But he responds:

> Whoever drinks this water
> will be thirsty again;
> but no one who drinks the water that I shall give him
> will ever be thirsty again:
> the water that I shall give him
> will become in him a spring of water, welling up for
>   eternal life. (John 4:13b-14 NJB)

Jesus is offering this woman something radically new, radically different. He is offering her a life whose energy comes from within, instead of having to be excited from without. He is offering her a freedom (as we see later in the dialogue) to be in touch with God anywhere, not just at one church or another. He is offering her a chance to be a source of happiness for others, instead of being entirely dependent on others for whatever happiness she knows.

All through this dialogue, as in the previous one with Nicodemus, the woman is not really sure where Jesus is leading her. But she allows herself to be led, to be feminine and receptive before the Lord, even as we all must be. Once, when she tries to be evasive, Jesus gently leads her back to the issue, which is the freedom of the Spirit that comes with acknowledging him as Lord. He calls her to a deeper level of being where she can let go of her illusions, her dependency, her hypocrisy. He loves her exactly where she is, and yet he continues to ask more of her.

Sometimes we forget that demanding dimension of love. Love is not the same as approval. If we truly love someone we want them to be everything they can and should be. We take the risk to call them out of their shallowness and into their depth. Those who truly love us likewise challenge us and call forth the best in us. They insist that we be more than we have been, they invite us to envision and embrace the possibility of growth, and they support us as we move into areas that are unfamiliar to us. The love of Jesus has this demanding quality to it.

In chapter 6 we see a perfect example of this. Jesus comes across a crippled man, and although his heart goes out to him, he does not cure him on the spot. Instead, he asks the man if he wants to be well again, and only after he says yes does the Lord agree to heal him.

Sometimes we prefer the comfort of our own crippledness to the riskiness of health. It is easier to keep living with our defenses and illusions than to tear them down and face the demands of life head on. We would rather be pitied than healed. The Lord does not want to leave us like that, but he will not do our growing for us. He will not heal us without our consent. We have to say yes to his demanding love and allow ourselves to be led by him from sin to grace, from death to life. Only then will we experience his gracious love in retrospect.

The Sign of Life-Giving Bread

Responding to the Lord's invitation to new life is always finally rewarding, but it is not initially obvious. In chapter 6 Jesus challenges the perception of those who would follow him by telling them:

> In all truth I tell you,
> if you do not eat the flesh of the Son of man
> and drink his blood,
> you have no life in you.
> Anyone who does eat my flesh and drink my blood
> has eternal life,
> and I shall raise that person up on the last day.
> (John 6:53-54 JB)

This long discourse on Jesus as the bread of life is one of those gospel passages which probably reflects a concern of the early Church rather than an actual event in the life of Jesus. Yet John knows the teaching of the Lord. He knows this is the understanding of the Eucharist which Jesus bequeathed to his disciples. He knows that this is the teaching of the Church, the body of Christ, in his own day. And since he knows this is the Lord's teaching, he shows the Lord teaching it in this gospel.

When we read this passage, therefore, we should see the characters as people who, in John's time, were feeling challenged by the Church's teaching on the Eucharist. Of course we do not have to limit it to those people; Christians in our own day have to face this teaching of the Lord and either accept it or reject it. They can identify with the disciples in the story who say, "This sort of talk is intolerable. How could anyone take it seriously?" (John 6:60).

Jesus knows full well what is bothering them. But what does he do? Does he try to explain the mystery to them? Does he offer them a theological interpretation? No, he says simply:

It is the spirit that gives life,
the flesh has nothing to offer.
The words I have spoken to you are spirit
and they are life. (John 6:63 NJB)

In other words, Jesus asks his followers simply to take him at his word. It is only by accepting the mystery of what he is saying that they can experience the reality of what he is talking about.

Jesus could just as well have said, "Look, there's no way that you're going to be able to comprehend this mystery! Just accept it because I've asked you to. I want you to believe that in giving you this bread and wine I am giving you myself. If you do that, you will find me really present in the Eucharist, whether or not you can explain it."

Too often in Christian history we have wasted time trying to explain the Eucharist. But nobody can ever fully explain a mystery. Who today can completely explain the human mystery of falling in love? Why then should we think we ought to be able to explain a divine mystery?

Understanding how Christ becomes present to us in the Eucharist is not our problem. It's God's problem. But we do not have to solve God's problem. We have only to accept his promise to be present to us in the breaking of the bread and the sharing of the wine. Once we do that, once we say yes to his promise of self-giving, we open ourselves up to the possibility of experiencing the divine presence.

Unlike people in the East, Western culture has always had a hard time dealing with mystery. We have a philosophical bias against accepting anything unless we can explain it. We do not want to accept that there may be mysteries we do not understand, that there may be problems we cannot solve.

God, however, is not a problem to be solved, but a mystery to be lived. And a mystery is not a puzzle to be taken apart and put back together, but a truth so large that we can only touch one part of it at a time. We have to let ourselves encounter it bit by bit, knowing some aspects of it through our involvement in the mystery, without expecting that we will ever comprehend the whole picture. We can never grasp a mystery; we can only allow ourselves to be grasped by it.

That kind of surrender, that kind of letting go is needed if we are ever to receive the gift of Jesus' presence in the Eucharist. For we cannot make Jesus present to us. We cannot manipulate the Lord. We can only say yes, we are ready for it, if God will grant it to us. As Jesus says to his disciples, "No one can come to me unless it is granted by the Father" (John 6:65).

Looking around, Jesus sees that some of his would-be followers are not ready for that degree of surrender. They are not ready for that depth of faith, for they begin to walk away from him. Others join them. You can almost see the sadness in his eyes as he watches them start down the road without him.

> Then Jesus turned to the twelve and asked, "Do you want to leave me, too?" Simon Peter answered for them, "Lord, where would we go? You alone have the words of eternal life." (John 6:67-68)

That's a prayer that many of us can identify with. Sometimes we are not certain what our lives mean. Sometimes we cannot say for sure that we're going in any direction. At times like that we may admit to the Lord that he does not seem real to us. We may confess that we have our own doubts and we would like to give up. And yet we have to say to him in all honesty: Where else could we go? We have experienced his goodness in the past. His words have led us to life before. The memory of graces past gives us the courage to keep walking with him, even when there are no miracles happening, even when we desperately need one.

Do you remember how Jesus promised living water to the woman at the well in chapter 4? At that point in the gospel, the evangelist did not explain the enigmatic "living water." But now in chapter 7 John makes it clear that the living water is the Holy Spirit. Jesus cries out in the temple:

> "Let those who are thirsty come to me! Let them come and drink, if they believe in me! For it is in the scriptures that rivers of living water shall flow from God." Jesus was speaking of the Spirit, which those who came to believe in him were to receive. But they did not have the Spirit yet, because Jesus had not yet been glorified. (John 7:37-39)

When we are filled with the Spirit, it's a glorious experience. But once we believe in Jesus and receive the Spirit, he is with us even though we do not feel it. All we need to do is thirst for him and trust in him, and he will give us the courage to continue. The Spirit will give us life when we need it, and it will give us life in abundance when we are able to receive it.

For the evangelist, Jesus is the perfect example of living in the Spirit. He is always filled with courage. He is always sure of himself. He is always certain of his divinity and his mission. If all we had was John's gospel, we would have no sense that Jesus might have grown in self-awareness. We would have no suspicion that Jesus might have come gradually to the realization of his origin and destiny. The Jesus of John's gospel is the glorified Christ. He is the Jesus of post-resurrection reality. He is the Lord who is encountered in prayer and received in the Eucharist. And so this gospel is filled with images of the truly larger-than-life Jesus.

Signs and Images of Jesus

As we have seen in the prologue, Jesus is the Word of God. In the chapters of the gospel just discussed, he is the bread of life and the source of the Spirit for all believers. In the chapters which follow these, Jesus is portrayed in further images which have become very familiar to us through the years.

In chapter 8 Jesus is proclaimed as the "light of the world":

I am the light of the world;
anyone who follows me will not be walking in the
dark
but will have the light of life. (John 8:12b NJB)

Here Jesus is stating openly who he is, and John uses statements such as this one to build up the antagonism between Jesus and the unbelieving Jews. John knows that those religious leaders were ultimately responsible for the death of Jesus, and like all the gospel writers he must show how disbelief and nonacceptance led inevitably to the crucifixion. In this chapter this self-proclamation of Jesus leads to a dispute between himself and the Pharisees.

The dispute continues in the next chapter. Jesus not only says that he is the light of the world, but he gives a sign that shows it. He restores the sight of a man who has been blind from birth, dispelling his darkness and giving him light. But since Jesus healed the blind man on the sabbath, the Pharisees are furious.

John narrates this beautiful story in such a way that it becomes a parable of faith. The blind man comes to Jesus and he is healed. He rejoices in his newly found sight, but others refuse to accept the fact that it was Jesus who brought new light into his life. Out of their own darkness they drive him away, but when he meets Jesus again he falls to his knees and worships him as Lord.

At one level John is telling his community that they can expect people to persecute them for rejoicing in the light which Jesus has brought into their lives and that they should not give in to the forces of darkness. At another level, however, John is teaching the readers of his gospel that we are all born blind. We could very easily remain in darkness like the Pharisees if, in our pride, we claim to be self-sufficient. And if we are too sure that we have it all, we surely don't.

As the gospel continues, each chapter builds upon the

preceding one. Each chapter gives us another image of who Jesus is for those who believe in him and know him as Lord.

In chapter 10 Jesus describes himself as "the good shepherd," as one who knows each of those who is entrusted to his care. Unlike a hired hand, a good shepherd does not run away when danger comes, but he puts his own life on the line for the sake of his flock. He leads his sheep to green pastures and gives them all that they need; in return, they know and love the shepherd.

John is portraying the relationship between Christ and his people in an image of total dedication and mutual recognition. Obviously, the risen Christ knows and loves the Church and every person in it. Obviously, the earthly Christ sacrificed his life so that others might live. But it is not always so obvious that those in the Church are good sheep! John is presuming that each of the sheep knows the shepherd personally and appreciates all that he does for them. So the relationship is mutual between the shepherd and the flock: They know and love each other personally.

But is this always true in our Churches? Can we honestly say that everyone in our parishes allows Jesus to be their shepherd? Do they just call him the good shepherd, or have they really experienced his leadership in their lives? John here is pointing out that our relationship to Christ has to be just as personal as his relationship to us. Just because we are sheep doesn't mean we belong to his flock!

Another image presented later in the gospel emphasizes this mutuality between Christ and the Church even more vividly:

> I am the vine and you are the branches. If you share
> in my life and I share in yours, you will bear much
> fruit; but cut off from me you can do nothing.
> (John 15:5)

Here it is clear that the connection between Christ and each Christian has to be intimate in order to be life-giving. Unless we cultivate and maintain a close relationship to Christ in prayer, we cannot claim to be personally related to him. Just because we are branches doesn't mean we are attached to the vine!

The Sign of Resurrection

All through the first part of this gospel, the Book of Signs, John has been showing how Christ is a victorious Lord: he overcomes darkness and blindness, ignorance and misunderstanding, hatred and fear, hunger and thirst, sickness and disease. Finally, in chapter 11, he shows that Christ is triumphant over the ultimate obstacle of every human being's desire for life. Christ is victorious even over death: He is resurrection and life itself.

The story of the raising of Lazarus is not found in any of the other gospels. It is unique to John, for it highlights John's unique understanding of the universal Lordship of Christ. It portrays Jesus as both very human and nonetheless divine. He has friends whom he loves very much. His heart is moved by the tears of Martha and Mary for their dead brother, and he himself weeps when he comes in sight of Lazarus's tomb. But at the same time, he knows why he has come to the tomb. He knows he has come to give glory to the Father, and to show that God's power is within him. And he knows he has come to give the ultimate sign of his Lordship.

The dialogue here, like the earlier dialogues in this gospel, gradually moves into deeper and deeper revelations of the mystery of Christ. At one point,

> Martha said to Jesus, "Lord, if you had been here, my brother would not have died. And even now, if you ask God for anything, I am sure he will grant it." Jesus assured her, "Your brother will rise again." She replied, "I know he will rise again, at the resurrection on the last day."
> Then Jesus said, "I am the resurrection and the life. All those who believe in me will live, even if they have died. And all those who live and believe in me will never die." (John 11:21-26)

Jesus is saying that to live in him is to know a life so real that it can never be taken away, not even by death. And to carry this life within is to know that it will go on, even after death.

But it is not easy to believe this when face to face with the apparent finality of death. So Jesus asks Martha if she really believes this, and she responds in a way which reveals the depth of her faith:

> "Yes, Lord, I have come to believe that you are the Christ, the Son of God, the one who was to come into the world." (John 11:27)

Mary comes to join them, and the two sisters lead Jesus to the place where Lazarus has been laid. The tomb symbolizes the deadness, the coldness, the hardness in every life which makes it seem much more like death. This is the sin which Jesus approaches when he asks to be admitted to the human heart. This is the sin of the world which the lamb of God has come to take away. And so Jesus asks those nearby to roll away the stone at the entrance of the tomb. He has come to shed his light in the darkness, to overcome deadness with his life.

Notice that Jesus does not roll away the stone by his own power. Undoubtedly he could do it by himself, and yet he invites others to participate with him in the miracle of giving life. As if to emphasize this, he does it again at the very moment when he gives the most powerful sign of his divinity. He calls to the man inside the tomb:

> "Lazarus, come out!" The dead man came out, his hands and feet wrapped in strips, his face covered by a cloth. Then Jesus said, "Unbind him, and let him go free." (John 11:43-44)

John's teaching here, masterfully described in this symbolic action of Jesus at the tomb, is that the Lord alone gives life, and yet he also needs us to help him. The risen Lord cannot work miracles unless a community of believers is willing to share in the work of rolling away the stones which oppress people and take away their humanity. This is the meaning and the purpose of the Church: to participate with Jesus in overcoming the darkness of the world and liberating humanity for the truth of God.

In John's understanding of the good news, Christians are not called to just a Jesus-and-me relationship. It is not enough for us to be individually related to the Lord. Our personal relationship with Jesus must embrace others as well. Even though Jesus wants to enter every tomb, only we can roll away the stone for him. Even though he wants to give life to every person, only we can undo the bonds which restrict their freedom.

Community is not something which is added on to the Christian life; it is at the very heart of that life. Christianity is a way for people to live community. The power of the gospel is felt mainly in reciprocal relationships based on cooperation instead of domination, vulnerability instead of righteousness. Jesus' power to heal is experienced most strongly in relationships which heal the brokenness of individuals who are isolated from one another.

With chapter 12 the Book of Signs comes to an end, and yet it ends not with community but with isolation. The unbelieving Jews do not accept the signs that Jesus has worked in their midst. They refuse to let themselves be drawn into the life which Jesus wants to share with them and which he invites them to share with others. Like all those who hear the good news and do not accept it, they choose the glamour of the world over the glory of the Lord. They choose to be alone rather than to unite themselves with life. They stand condemned to isolation with the prince of darkness, while Jesus prepares to reveal himself as the light of the world to all those who will come to him:

> The world is now being sentenced, and the prince of this world will be overthrown. When I am lifted up from the earth, I shall draw everyone to myself....I am the light which has come into the world, so that all those who believe in me do not have to stay in darkness. (John 12:31-32, 46)

The Book of Glory: Lordship Revealed

In the first half of John's gospel we are told time and again that "the hour has not yet come" (John 2:4; 7:30; 8:20). What is this enigmatic "hour"?

Now, at the beginning of the second half, we are told:

As the feast of Passover approached, Jesus knew that the hour had come for him to pass from this world to the Father. (John 13:1)

Four days before this, Jesus had seen it coming, for he said:

The hour is finally approaching for the son of man to be glorified. (John 12:23)

This "hour," then, is the time for Jesus to enter into his glory. Yet in John's gospel Jesus makes his entrance in a most inglorious manner. There is no triumphant procession into Jerusalem. There is no Passover celebration with his disciples. Instead, he takes his last supper with his friends on the day before Passover, the day when the paschal lambs are slaughtered for the festival. All this is symbolic in John's gospel, and yet it symbolizes the reality which all the gospels reveal: that the way into the Father's kingdom is through serving others, even to the point of suffering and dying for them.

Glory in Service

The first scene in the Book of Glory, therefore, shows Jesus wrapping a towel around his waist, kneeling down in front of his own disciples, and washing their feet. "What is he doing?" we can ask with the disciples. And yet we know what he is doing. He is showing his disciples how to enter into glory. It is not by working miracles; it is not by seeking people's praise; it is by serving humbly, caring for others, doing the Father's work where only the Father can see.

Characteristically, Peter does not understand this at all!

He refuses to let Jesus wash his feet, so Jesus has to make it clear to him what is at stake. He tells Peter plainly, "If I do not wash you, you are not really with me." So Peter gets the message, and as usual, he accepts it with his whole heart: "Lord, then don't wash just my feet. Wash my face and hands as well!" (John 13:8-9).

Even so, Peter does not fully comprehend. But for now, he does not have to. For now, it is enough that he understands what Jesus says next to the disciples:

> If I as Lord and teacher have washed your feet, then you should wash each other's feet. I have given you an example so that you might do what I have done for you. (John 13:14-15)

Glory in Communion

And so John's account of the last supper begins. It is quite different from the last supper narratives in the other three gospels. For one thing, it is quite long, covering over four chapters, which is one-fifth of the entire gospel. The synoptic gospels each fit the last supper into a part of one chapter. For another thing, John does not relate the institution of the Eucharist, whereas in the synoptics this is the main focus of Jesus' last meal with his 12 closest disciples.

Scholars have proposed various explanations for this omission of the Eucharist in the fourth gospel. One is that since it was written last, John did not feel obliged to mention what the other three gospels clearly taught. Another is that since John presented his theology of the Eucharist in the bread of life discourse in chapter 6, he saw no need to repeat it here. But if we read the last supper discourse in John's gospel and meditate on the words of Jesus, we find that even though the Eucharist itself is never mentioned, this whole scene is like a long meditation on the meaning of the Eucharist.

One meaning of the Eucharist is thanksgiving. The Greek word *eucharistia* primarily means "thankfulness" or "thanksgiving." And all through this discourse we hear Jesus giving thanks to the Father and returning the glory God has given him. For example, the discourse begins:

> Now has the Son of Man been glorified,
> and in him God has been glorified.
> If God has been glorified in him,
> God will in turn glorify him in himself,
> and will glorify him very soon. (John 13:31b-32 NJB)

Note how John is also teaching here that the glorification of the Son at the same time gives glory to the Father.

Another meaning of the Eucharist is sacrifice—sacrifice in the sense of self-giving, self-offering and service to others. We have already seen that the theme of the very first scene of the last supper is service to one another. In this discourse John is often meditating on the sacrifice of Jesus, on the meaning of his self-offering to the Father, to whom he is about to return. More than once, Jesus says explicitly to the disciples who are sad at the thought of his leaving them, "Do not be sad, for I am going to the Father" (John 14:1-3, 13, 27-28).

A third important meaning of the Eucharist is unity. Jesus speaks often of his unity with the Father, and he reminds his disciples of his unity with them in the image of the vine and the branches (John 15:1-8).

In the end, the all-embracing meaning of the Eucharist is love, and Jesus' farewell discourse is filled with words of love. He speaks eloquently of the love between himself and the Father, of his love for his disciples, and of their love for one another. One of the most beautiful passages in this discourse shows how these three dimensions of love are blended together:

> I have loved you
> just as the Father has loved me.
> Remain in my love.
> If you keep my commandments,
> you will remain in my love,
> just as I have kept my Father's commandments
> and remain in his love.
> I have told you this
> so that my own joy may be in you

and your joy be complete.
This is my commandment:
love one another,
as I have loved you.
No one can have greater love
than to lay down his life for his friends.

(John 15:9-13 JB)

What follows in chapters 18 and 19 is well known. Jesus lays down his life for his friends and offers up his life to his Father. But at the same time, he lays down his life for everyone, so that all may have life in him—and right away we see the implication of that. In his ultimate act of self-giving, Jesus is giving the ultimate sign that everyone is his friend. He stretches out his arms on the cross to embrace all of us, to befriend each and every one of us. Jesus prayed at the last supper:

I pray not only for these,
but also for those
who through their teachings will come to believe in
   me.
May they all be one.
just as, Father, you are in me and I am in you,
so that they also may be in us,
so that the world may believe it was you who sent
   me. (John 17:20-21 JB)

Glory in Forgiveness

Just as there is no institution scene at the last supper, so also there is no resurrection scene in John's gospel. Once again, it is as though John bypasses the event in order to meditate on its meaning. In chapter 20 all we find is the empty tomb, but shortly after that, Jesus finds his disciples to tell them what his resurrection means for them.

Peace be with you.
As the Father sent me,
so I am sending you....

Receive the Holy Spirit.
If you forgive anyone's sins,
they are forgiven;
If you retain anyone's sins,
they are retained. (John 20:21b-23 JB)

With resurrection comes peace. With resurrection comes reassurance of the Father's mission. With resurrection comes the power of the Holy Spirit. Jesus gives to his disciples the same spirit that empowered him from the very beginning. They now have the same mission which he had from the Father. They share in the calm assurance of their own sonship, and their commission is to bring that same peace to others.

And how is that peace to be spread? It is through forgiveness and acceptance and reconciliation. It is not by conquest. It is not by domination. It is not by exercising power over others. Rather, it is by exercising the Spirit's power to love and to forgive even those who are unlovable and unforgivable, just as Jesus did. That is something geniunely new. When God's forgiving love is in our relationships with others, we give to them the same peace which the incarnate Lord bestowed on his disciples.

In the very last chapter of John's gospel we see what Jesus means by giving peace through forgiveness. If there was one disciple who needed to be reassured of Jesus' love for him, it was Peter. As we saw in Matthew's gospel, Peter professed his faith in Jesus, but he began to sink beneath the waves when his faith faltered. In John's gospel, Peter says he will not leave the Lord, that he wants to be washed head to foot in relationship with Jesus. Yet when Jesus is arrested, Peter refuses to admit that he ever knew the man.

The synoptic gospels tell us that Peter wept bitterly over what he had done, but John does not mention that at all. Instead, the risen Jesus prepares a meal for his disciples. Afterwards he three times asks Peter (who had denied him three times) if he loves him. You can just see the remorse in Peter's eyes as he says, "Lord, you know everything! You know I love you!" (John 21:17).

Peter realizes that he is forgiven because Jesus trusts him

with the very task he was just symbolically performing for Peter. Jesus tells him, "Feed my lambs....Feed my sheep." The Lord loves Peter into being the disciple that he always wanted to be.

So Peter is finally ready to accept Jesus' mission from the Father as his own. He is ready to be Christ in a world which fears the love of Christ. When he is forgiven, he can let go of the shame and guilt which would have driven him back to the life of an unknown Galilean fisherman.

Seeing this, Jesus says to Peter:

> In all truth I tell you,
> when you were young
> you put on your own belt
> and walked where you liked;
> but when you grow old
> you will stretch out your hands,
> and somebody else will put a belt around you
> and take you where you would rather not go.
>
> (John 21:18 JB)

At last, Peter understands the Lordship of Jesus. The cost of discipleship is your whole life. And the reward of discipleship is your whole life.

CHAPTER THREE

Luke and Acts:
The Gift of the Spirit

When we think of the New Testament today, we think mainly of gospels and epistles. We might even take it for granted that a Christian author in the first century would naturally have written one or the other. But Luke did something different. He wrote a long story about the origins of Christianity, beginning with the birth of Jesus in Palestine and ending with the proclamation of his Lordship in the city of Rome. He wanted to show how the salvation of the world had spread from an obscure village on the outskirts of civilization to the very heart of the Roman Empire.

The two main parts of Luke's lengthy work were later separated from one another. The first part was grouped with the synoptic gospels, and the second part was placed between John's gospel and Paul's epistles. When we read the two parts separated from one another, however, we miss the dynamic continuity of the whole work.

That large picture in Luke's mind looked something like this: The Holy Spirit enters into human history through Mary's assent to be the mother of the savior. When Jesus reaches manhood, the Spirit leads him to the desert to be tempted; then, anointing him with power, the Spirit sends him to preach from Galilee to Judea, moving always closer to Jerusalem, the heart of Israel. There he is rejected by the Jewish leaders, crucified and buried, but God raises him up and the Holy Spirit encourages his disciples to spread the good news of the resurrection. At every major turn in the early Church's journey, the Spirit is there, guiding the community and empowering its members to bring the message of Christ to all people. Eventually, the Spirit inspires Paul to bring the news of Jesus to the gentiles; he traveled three times around the empire and finally to Rome itself.

Luke did not name this long work, but it could have easily been called the Book of the Holy Spirit. It is the story of the Spirit's entrance into human history and of its transforming presence in the world. Jesus is himself filled with the power of the Spirit. Then, at the end of what we today call the Gospel According to Luke, Jesus tells his followers, "Stay in the city until you are covered by the power from on high" (Luke 24:49). In what was later named the Acts (meaning "deeds" or "activities") of the Apostles, the Spirit descends upon the gathered community on the feast of Pentecost. Suddenly, there is a new vitality in the Church, a new source of power and growth which causes it to burst into the world and proclaim God's message of salvation. Just as Jesus was empowered by the Holy Spirit, now the followers of Jesus are empowered by the same Spirit. It teaches them how to live in the Spirit, and it attracts people of the whole world to that redeemed and redemptive life-style.

The author of this early chronicle of the power of the Holy Spirit was not one of the original disciples. He was a gentile convert to Christianity who apparently was a traveling companion of Paul during some of his missionary journeys. Paul mentions him in one of his letters (Colossians 4:14), and there are three sections in Acts where the author suddenly slips into speaking of "us" rather than "them," suggesting that Luke was writing about things that he personally remembered.

Various hints within his writing suggest that Luke gathered all his sources together and composed his work between the years 70 and 90. Other clues tell us that he was writing for a non-Jewish audience. An ancient tradition describes him as a doctor from Antioch in Syria, and some scripture commentators have noted passages where Luke seems to describe things with the eye of a physician.

Luke the writer, however, was more concerned with spiritual healing than with medical healing. His perspective

72

might be called a theology of salvation, an awareness of how people are being healed and of how the world is being redeemed through the message of Jesus and the power of the Holy Spirit.

Luke's gospel and the Acts together are the longest work by a single author in the New Testament. Rather than examining it scene by scene, as we have with the other gospels, we will look at it from the point of view of Luke's theology, his understanding of salvation and redemption. We will begin with his account of the Spirit's work in Jesus' life, and then move on to his description of the Spirit in the early Church.

The Gospel According to Luke

Like the evangelist Matthew, Luke opens his gospel with an account of Jesus' birth. Luke's infancy account, however, says much about Mary which can be treated better separately (see Chapter Four). Let us begin here, then, with Luke's account of the ministry of Jesus in the power of the Holy Spirit.

Three times at the beginning of Jesus' public ministry, Luke explicitly mentions the gift of the Holy Spirit. When Jesus is baptized in the Jordan, the Spirit descends on him in the form of a dove (Luke 3:22). Immediately afterwards, Jesus is filled with the Spirit and led into the wilderness to face temptation (Luke 4:1). Then Jesus returns to Galilee with the power of the Holy Spirit in him, proclaiming the good news (Luke 4:14).

In Matthew and Mark the good news is the nearness of God's kingdom. For Luke, while the meaning of the good news is the same, he says it differently. He speaks not of God's kingdom but of God's justice, and he especially emphasizes the privileged position of the poor. Luke is sometimes called the "gospel of the poor and lowly" or the "gospel of mercy." He stresses the freedom and liberation which comes from living simply and humbly, in right relationship with others, under the reign of God. He sees Jesus as fulfilling the prophesy of Isaiah 61:

> The spirit of the Lord is on me,
> for he has anointed me
> to bring the good news to the afflicted.

He has sent me to proclaim liberty to captives,
sight to the blind,
to let the oppressed go free,
to proclaim a year of favour from the Lord.
(Luke 4:18-19a NJB)

The Good News of God's Justice

When we think of justice, we ordinarily think of a balance: If the scales tip too much on the side of wrong, justice is needed to set things right. Moreover, we know we're not perfect; we know we've done wrong. So we envision God's justice as coming along to straighten out the mess we've made. Our image is often some form of retribution projected onto God: If we've put ourselves up, God will pull us down a few pegs. If we've taken something unjustly, God will make us give it back. If we've been having too much fun, God will restore the balance and make us suffer. And that idea of God's justice is really *bad news*.

But that is not the biblical concept of divine justice. According to the scriptures, God is just when he is being true to himself. God is the scale of justice. God's justice is not the opposite of God's mercy, as we have sometimes thought. In God, all things are one, all things are reconciled. God's justice is the same as his mercy; it is identical with his love. And God's love, as we have seen all through the Old Testament, is forgiving, steadfast and unconditional. So God's justice is God acting in accordance with what he is, which is love.

Luke's gospel is filled with images of God's justice in the scriptural sense. Jesus eats with sinners and the outcasts of society because "It is not those who are well that need a doctor, but the sick. I have not come to invite the upright to change, but the ones who have fallen short of the mark" (Luke 5:31-32). Luke tells the story of the repentant prostitute who washes Jesus' feet with her tears and wipes them with her hair: "Her many sins must have been forgiven because she shows such great love" (Luke 7:47). He tells about the unscrupulous tax collector named Zacchaeus, who is so grateful for Jesus' honoring him with a visit that he promises to become an honest man (Luke 19:1-10). When people are touched by God's justice and love, they themselves become just and loving. Only Luke's gospel contains these special stories of God's forgiving justice.

In chapter 15 Luke gives us three memorable parables of God's mercy. Jesus tells of the shepherd who rejoices at finding a lost sheep, of the woman who rejoices at finding a lost coin (note the feminine image of God), of the father who rejoices at the return of his prodigal son. These are all images of a loving God being true to himself. They are all images of God's justice.

As we can see from these examples, God's justice requires that he go out of himself and extend himself, his love, to others. The shepherd doesn't just wait till the stupid sheep wanders back. The woman doesn't just forget about the coin till it shows up. The father doesn't just go about his business; he watches the road every day till his son returns so he can go out to welcome him home. God's love is relentlessly just: He never gives up on those who have forgotten his love.

The parable of the prodigal son reminds us of another image of God's justice which is found in other gospels as well as Luke's. It is the image of the banquet which the forgiving father throws to celebrate the son's return. Since the days of the exile, the Jews had envisioned the redemption of Israel as a sumptuous banquet provided by Yahweh for his starving people. Nobody would be turned away; everyone would have their fill (Isaiah 55:1-2). All of the evangelists show how this came true in Jesus' ministry with the feeding of the 5,000 from a few loaves and fishes (Luke 9:10-17).

But Luke also points out that being invited to the banquet is not enough: We have to let go of our other concerns and accept the invitation. In Luke's day it was the Jews, those to whom the messianic banquet had been promised, who had missed the feast by rejecting Jesus (Luke 13:25-30). He tells the parable of the guests who are invited to a wedding feast, but who turn it down because they are too busy with their own affairs. So the master of the house sends his servants out to bring in everyone that they can find: the beggars and derelicts, the cripples and the blind (Luke 14:15-24). We see that it is the little ones who are ready to recognize and enjoy God's gifts.

We often think that justice means getting what we deserve, but the gospels point out that God's justice always gives us more than we deserve. In fact, "worthiness" is not even the issue! Matthew tells the parable of a landowner who hires men in the morning, at noon and in the afternoon to work in his fields. In the evening when he pays them all a day's wages, the ones who worked all day complain that they deserve more than the ones who worked only a few hours. But the landowner turns to them and asks, "Why are you looking so resentful just because I am generous?" (Matthew 20:15). God's justice is really magnanimity, being more than fair to everybody because he is being true to himself. As Matthew says elsewhere, God makes the sun to shine and the rain to fall on the just and the unjust alike (Matthew 5:45). In other words, he gives everyone all that they need in order to grow.

We have a hard time with that kind of justice. We are capitalists, even in the spiritual life. We're more comfortable with an eye for an eye and a tooth for a tooth. We don't know what to do with a God who breaks that rule! Yet God's justice is just another way of thinking about God's unconditional love. All through Luke's gospel people are receiving what they don't deserve: An unknown Jewish girl is asked to be the mother of the messiah. Blue-collar workers are invited to be the first disciples of the Lord. People who are sick are cured. People whose lives are broken are healed. The starving are fed. The outcast are welcomed. The possessed are freed. The dead are raised to life. God's justice is on the loose!

That kind of relentless generosity is hard for us to comprehend, much less practice. That kind of unconditional justice is beyond our human power. Yet Luke is showing that it is possible to be fully human and divinely just. It is possible for Jesus because he lived in the power of the Spirit. Likewise it is possible for all those who, like Jesus, recognize that God is their Father and open themselves to receive his Spirit.

The Good News of Spiritual Power
It is the gift of the Holy Spirit, then, which enables Christ's disciples to be impossibly just (in this God-like sense) to everyone. It is by living in the Spirit that they can do what God does. Or as Jesus puts it, "Be compassionate, just the way your Father is compassionate" (Luke 6:36). It is by the power of the

Spirit that they can do what others cannot:

> Love your enemies; do good to those who hate you.
> Bless those who curse you; pray for those who treat
> you badly. If someone slaps you on one cheek, let
> him slap the other one. If someone takes your coat,
> let him take your shirt as well. Treat others the way
> you want them to treat you. (Luke 6:27-30)

The gift of the Spirit is thus God's own power to love unconditionally—and to transform the world by that power. It is the power of faith, to believe in miracles and see them happen (Luke 17:5-6). It is the power which the disciples began to share in, even during Jesus' lifetime. At one point, Jesus sends dozens of them out into the hill towns to do what he has been doing, and they discover that they too have the power of the Spirit:

> The seventy-two came back exuberant. "Lord," they
> told him, "even the demons obey us when we
> command them in your name!" (Luke 10:17)

Yet it is not all triumph and glory. Jesus warns his disciples that, for the sake of the gospel, they may find themselves homeless (Luke 9:58), rejected by others (Luke 10:10) and causing dissension (Luke 12:52-53). Whenever things look like they're going well for Jesus, he tells his followers that ultimately he is going toward the cross (Luke 9:22; 10:44; 18:31-33), and he makes it clear that he expects no less from them:

> If you want to follow me, you have to forget about
> yourself, take up your cross every day, and go the
> way that I go. If you want to save your life you're
> going to lose it, but if you lose your life on account
> of me, you will really save it. (Luke 10:23-24)

The gift of the Spirit, then, is not only the power of unconditional love, it is also the power of unconditional trust. It is the power that enables Jesus to believe in his Father's love as he faces the darkest passage of his ministry. On the night before he is to die, he shares one last supper with his closest friends. Luke's account shows Jesus trusting in his Father even though he is well aware of what is coming:

> When it was time to eat, he took his place at the table with the apostles. He said to them, "I really wanted to share this passover meal with you before I have to suffer, since I will not partake of it again till what it signifies is fulfilled in the kingdom of God."
>
> (Luke 22:14-16)

Power to Embrace Suffering

After that first Eucharist, Jesus goes to pray on the Mount of Olives, asking his friends to pray with him. We know the scene so well. We know how the disciples all fell asleep. We know the words that are recorded in the gospel as he put his life into his Father's hands. We can also imagine that during that long night of solitary prayer, he said more than the few words which have been recorded for us. Maybe they went something like this:

> God, if I am your friend, why do I have to go through with this? Lord, if I am your chosen one, why do I have to be treated this way? Father, if I am your son, isn't there another way to be a son of God?
>
> If there is any other way that I can be true to myself and true to you, if there is any possible way but the one I see before me, show it to me now. Take the pain and agony away from me. Take the senselessness of it away from me.
>
> I don't understand how this absurd event will do any good for anyone! I don't see how my own death can give anyone life! Shouldn't I be able to know how it will all turn out? Why should I have to trust you, even to the end?
>
> Still, if this is the path that you have chosen for me, I will take it. If this is the cup that you have given to me, I will drink it. If this is the meaning which your word is speaking in my heart, let it be. If this is

the purpose which your design has planned for me, let it be. Even though I do not understand it, let it be. I want you, my Father, more than I want myself.

We see a very human Jesus in the garden. The Lord was fully human, and he would have felt what any man or woman would be feeling when facing a death that might be avoided. And so he spends his night of absolute aloneness with nothing but the power of the Spirit to sustain him. Everything else has been taken away. Even his friends are not with him. There's no human reason that he should believe that at this moment he is the Son of God, beloved of the Father.

And yet he knows one thing: the unconditional love of the God he has dared to call *Abba*. So now he stands on that. And with the sustaining power of God's Spirit, and with that alone, he moves into the night of faith.

We can understand this, too, once we have experienced the light which the Father's love gives to our lives. God's love is like the light that radiates from the sun: always shining in all directions, always pouring down upon our world. Yet sometimes it is cloudy, sometimes it is night. Sometimes we are cold, and we feel very much alone.

At times like that, we are inclined to say that the sun is not shining. But that's impossible! The sun cannot be the sun and not be shining. Even if we do not feel the warmth of its rays, we have to admit that it is still shining above the clouds, or on the other side of the globe.

It's exactly like that with the Father's love. There is no time or place that God is not a loving Father. There is no way that God could ever stop loving and still be God. Even when we do not feel the love, God is still loving us. Even when the darkness of absurdity hides the love from us, God is still loving us. Maybe something has come between us and the warmth of his love. Maybe we have turned around and can no longer see the light of that love. But God has not stopped being love.

In those times of darkness, when we do not see the sun, we have to keep believing in it. And in those times of loneliness, when we do not feel God's love, we have to keep trusting in it.

There is no other way. Jesus sees this in his agony in the garden, and so he lets himself be captured by those who consider him their enemy.

They lead him where he'd rather not go. Yet he goes willingly. His captors think that *they* are leading him, but he is following the lead of his Father. He is following the only way there is to overcome the evil of the world. He is overcoming it the way that God is showing him, step by painful step. He is letting his life be taken away from him, trusting in the promise of the resurrection.

So all the time when he is being beaten, he is standing on the truth that God is love. When he is being denied his rights, he is affirming his right to love. When he is being condemned to death, he is saying yes to everlasting love. He is loving with the Father's love, relentless and free, not surrendering to hatred, but overcoming the evil which tries to drag him down to disbelief and despair.

Power to Freely Love

The real irony of the crucifixion is not that Christ the King is crowned with thorns. It is that Jesus is the only free person in the whole scene! He is the captive, and yet he is not captured by the situation. He responds to their violence in perfect nonviolence and peace. In the power of the Holy Spirit he endures his pain in human darkness, yet still believes in the light. He dispels the human evil all around him with the divine goodness that shines within him.

Humanly, he is weak. His arms are stretched out on the wood, and his hands are nailed to the cross. He is lifted up for all to see. He has nothing to protect him. He is naked for everyone to laugh at. And yet he is the strongest person there, for he is the only one who is still strong enough to love. He is clothed with a power which the world, for all its strength, can never know.

Humanly, he has every reason in the world to hate those who are crucifying him. And he could easily resent those who deserted him, the ones he preached to, the ones he cured, the ones who called themselves his disciples and his friends. But he resists the temptation to hate. He refuses to be resentful.

Hatred and resentment would only add to the darkness. Only light can overcome the darkness. Only love can overcome evil.

But how does love overcome evil? First, by not succumbing to it, by not returning tit for tat, by not answering evil with more evil. By refusing to play the game which pride and greed, fear and self-defense, anger and resentment start in human relationships, love brings that game to a halt.

Second, love overcomes evil by absorbing it, by loving it to death. By accepting the effects of evil into itself, by suffering and not causing others to suffer, by patiently enduring the pain which hate inflicts on human relationships, love absorbs the energy needed to keep the spiraling game of evil going. Love creates the space where evil can come to rest and die.

So Jesus does not try directly to attack evil. He is not trying to defeat the anger and the fear which are crucifying him. A frontal attack on evil never works, because we have to take on evil's own weapons to do that. He is leaving that to his Father, while still offering himself. He will let God do the work of redemption. He will let the Spirit renew the world. He cannot do that by himself alone. He is just one man, hanging on a cross. All he can do is love, right here, right now. All that he can do is love as much as it's possible for one man to love. All that he can do is love and forgive with all the love the Father has given him. In that strategy, he forever gives the Church its most potent form of renewal and revolution.

His arms are open to embrace the world which hated him for loving it. The world is in darkness. It cannot see the light. Yet Jesus sees so clearly that the ones who are tormenting him are blinded by the world's darkness. So he says: "Father, forgive them! They don't know what they're doing" (Luke 23:34).

He is reconciling the world within himself. He is receiving the world's darkness and giving it his light. He is setting all creation free to see the Father's light. He is lifted up so all can see what love can do to hatred, what goodness can do to evil. His humanity is perfectly united with divinity, as his human heart loves those who kill him, loving them the same way that God loves them.

Yet his human spirit is in agony as he suffers from the pain. He hangs there, saying, as it were:

81

Father, I don't really know what's happening. I don't really understand how all of this can really be your will for me. But I know your love, and I have been faithful to that. I know your life, and I have been true to that. I have trusted you up to this moment, and I will go on trusting you. I believe that you can bring life out of this death. I am confident that you can make this ugliness beautiful, that you can make this absurdity meaningful. Now it is all up to you. I have done everything I can. I hand it over. I give up control. I surrender.

Knowing, therefore, that he has done the Father's will up on the very end, he cries out in a loud voice: "Father, into your hands I commit my spirit!" (Luke 23:46).

In that moment, the redemption is accomplished. In that moment, thousands of years of preparation come to an end, and a new era begins. For in that moment, one tiny bit of humanity is given and taken totally. The chasm is bridged. From now on there is no ultimate separation between the human and the divine. The eldest of many brothers and sisters said his perfect yes. The alienation of the world from God has been in some small measure, yet irreversibly, overcome. And the Lord awaits the rest to freely follow.

Power to Redeem Humanity

Like God's first act of creation, Christ's act of re-creation is totally free. It is a free act of love and self-giving. It is an act which overcomes the darkness. It is an act of light.

But now our own humanity knows that such freedom is in fact possible. Before, on human power alone, it was impossible. Now, through the power of the Holy Spirit, it has become possible. What has happened once can happen again and again and again.

But it can only happen freely. It can only happen if it is freely chosen. A free choice cannot be commanded; it can only be invited. And so the invitation is extended to us now, to those who call themselves the followers of Jesus. God asks if we will let him be our *Abba* too, if we will trust him through the darkness to the light. But he will not make the decision for us. We can only enter into the free decision of Jesus by making our own free decision.

Yet something has changed, and changed irreversibly, in the moment of Jesus' total self-giving. He gave himself completely to others, embracing them as his own flesh and blood, choosing to be brother to every human being. But he also gave himself completely to the Father, and in doing that, he drew his innumerable brothers and sisters into the same relationship. One of our human brothers has said yes to sonship in a perfect and unique way, so now God becomes uniquely our Father. The universal fatherhood of God is no longer just an abstract thought, for in Jesus it has begun to be a concrete reality. The relationship of Son to Father has become humanly incarnate.

The raising up of Jesus is God's confirmation of this relationship. His resurrection is the promise and the guarantee for all those who, like Jesus, embrace God as *Abba*. Jesus is the design of our destiny, if we trust in God completely. Jesus is the pattern of our victory, if we choose to live and die like him. For in him we see that those who put their faith in God are never put to shame.

We often tend to think of Jesus raising himself up from the dead, but that is not the way Luke talks about it in Acts. When the apostles proclaim the good news, they say that God *raised* Jesus to life and glory at the right hand of the Father (Acts 2:32; 4:10; 7:55). The Pauline epistles speak about the resurrection in this way as well (Romans 8:11; 2 Corinthians 13:4; Galatians 1:2).

Yet John and some of the other epistles also speak of Jesus as rising from the dead rather than as being raised by the power of God (John 2:19-22; Colossians 1:18). (It is from these same sources that we receive the picture of Jesus as a pre-existing person, as Word or Lord, before his birth.) We must say, therefore, that the scriptures give us different pictures of the mystery of Christ, different attempts to describe his mysterious reality. No single description can capture what Christians have been trying to comprehend for almost 2,000 years.

The scriptures tell us that the resurrection is important

not just for Jesus but also for ourselves. We know our faith in God is not in vain because the Father raised up the one who trusted him completely. He is the firstborn of many brothers and sisters who move through the void, waiting for the Father's resurrection, hoping against all human hope for what only God can give (Romans 8:11; 2 Corinthians 4:14; Colossians 1:18).

Inevitably there is a Good Friday in every life. Very often it does not end quickly but lasts through Holy Saturday. Yet we know now just as surely that Easter Sunday will come. It's as certain as the morning dawn after the night. It's as certain as the resurrection which the apostles experienced. It's as certain as the paschal mystery which we discover in our own lives, once we learn from the scriptures what to look for, and once we learn from Jesus how to live through death to resurrection.

Every time we do it, though, we know it is not our own doing. All we do is let it happen. All we do is let it be. All that we can do, actually, is get ourselves out of the way (which always feels like death). After that, it is out of our hands.

Through that surrender of ourselves we enter into a freedom which is not of our own making. It is a freedom which is given to us, once we have given up the freedom which is ours to hold on to or give away. It is the freedom Jesus entered into fully when the Father raised him up to glory. Through the power of the Spirit, Jesus passed from limited presence to total presence, from individual existence to limitless, shareable existence. Through the power of that same Spirit, we too enter that freedom of the spirit which cannot be bound by human edges. Every time we surrender to the Father in the paschal mystery, we experience in some small part what Jesus knows in fullness.

The Acts of the Apostles

In the Gospel According to Luke, the first half of Luke's long work, the Holy Spirit is fully bestowed on a single individual who acts with God's power, speaks with God's authority and loves with God's love. Through the gift of the Spirit given to Jesus, God's justice is announced and demonstrated as Jesus travels from Galilee to Jerusalem freeing the sick from their illnesses, liberating the enslaved from their sins and enriching the poor with the good news of sharing in the messianic banquet.

Now, in the second half, the same Spirit is bestowed on a body of God's sons and daughters who surrender their own lives to the Father, giving themselves to one another and to the world for its salvation. They continue the work of redemption by proclaiming the good news of what the Father did in Jesus—and by living out that good news in their lives. Empowered by the Holy Spirit, they spread the words and deeds of Jesus through Jerusalem, then through Palestine, then through the Roman Empire, and finally to Rome itself.

The Spirit Energizes

At the beginning of the Acts of the Apostles, Luke recounts the Lord's instruction to the disciples that they should remain in Jerusalem until they have been baptized with, immersed in and filled by the Holy Spirit. He tells them:

> You will receive power when the Holy Spirit overcomes you, and then you will be my witnesses in Jerusalem, throughout Judea and Samaria, and even to the ends of the earth. (Acts 1:8)

In Luke's account we see Jesus promising that the Spirit will be given some time after the ascension. In John's gospel, however, we get a slightly different picture. In John 20:22 we see Jesus bestowing the Spirit shortly after the resurrection. Which picture is the correct one?

We can be bothered by questions of that sort until we remember that the gospel writers were not interested with giving historically accurate accounts of events. They were concerned with spiritual truth, and they used the facts of history as they recalled them, perhaps 30 or 40 or 50 years later, to describe the spiritual truth which was still present and alive among them.

The spiritual truth is this: There is a difference between knowledge on ice and knowledge on fire. There is a difference between hearing the gospel and being inspired by it. There is a difference between knowing about Jesus and knowing Jesus.

Even though we call them both faith, there is a difference between intellectual belief and real trust. There is a difference between sitting back and receiving the good news and stepping out in confidence to act on it. Only the second is biblical faith: when our walk matches our talk.

The Spirit teaches us this new walk. When Jesus died, the apostles didn't have it. They all deserted Jesus on the cross. They were demoralized. They lacked conviction. They had no aim or purpose. But shortly afterwards, we know, they were transformed. They were changed from within. They acted, lived and walked (not just thought) in a new way. Those lukewarm followers began to act like people on fire. Or as Acts describes them, they are "the people who are turning our whole world upside down" (Acts 17:6).

When did it actually happen? We don't really know. From the perspective of decades later, it must have seemed like it happened pretty quickly. John puts it shortly after the crucifixion. Luke collapses it into a single miraculous morning about a month and a half later. But we don't really know, historically speaking. All that we can do is gather some clues from the New Testament record as it has come down to us.

One thing that we do know is that it was not God who changed. As we have seen all through our study of the Old Testament, it is people who change in their awareness of God's presence, their understanding of God's promise, their experience of God's love, their trust in God's faithfulness and their acceptance of the power which God offers them.

It must have taken the disciples a little while at least to come to that new experience of God which we call the risen Lord. Mary Magdalene first experienced the risen Lord near the empty tomb, but she thought at first he was a gardener (John 20:11-17). Two disciples walked with him on the road to Emmaus, but they did not recognize him right away (Luke 24:13-32). By the third day, more of the apostles were experiencing the presence of the resurrected Christ in their midst, but they did not comprehend it, thinking it might even be a ghost (Luke 24:36-37).

Somehow it was the Jesus they had known, but somehow it was not. It was a real presence, yet ordinary eyes were not enough to recognize him. They had to see him with the eyes of faith. They needed to grow in faith until their experience of him was so real that it seemed they could touch him. They needed the power of the Spirit to know him as the risen Lord. They needed the gift of grace to perceive his divinity, and to believe in his unity with the Father.

It is that same gift which we need today. We see the world on the brink of blowing itself up with nuclear weapons, yet so often we are apathetic about it. We hear of wars and famines, yet so often we choose to ignore them. We look around and see our parishes asleep while people are leaving the Church by the thousands. We look within ourselves and see we do not really care for holiness. We just want to be left alone, not bothered by someone else—not even God—making demands on us. All of this is evidence of something missing in our lives. All of this is showing that we do not really know the Holy Spirit.

We say that we believe in the Holy Spirit, but our belief is often just knowledge on ice. It is not firsthand knowledge, experiential knowledge, knowledge on fire. True, the gift of the Spirit is given to us in Baptism. The offer of that gift is renewed in Confirmation. That gift is offered every time we read the scriptures, every time we say a prayer, every time we go to Mass. Yet the gift is worthless unless we receive it. It does us no good unless we accept it. Unless we take it into our hearts and let it change us, it is a belief that leaves us cold.

When we experience that icy paralysis in our lives, we are not much different from the disciples in the upper room after the ascension. The cold fear that gripped them after the crucifixion was melted by the warm, personal presence of the risen Jesus. For 40 days they enjoyed his company. For 40 days he showed them what the Spirit's power can do. But after a time they no longer felt the closeness of his presence. After a while it seemed that he had left them and returned to the Father.

Those of us who were in the Cincinnati community of New Jerusalem from its beginning can identify with that. At the start one person after another was coming to know the Lord, experience his presence, feel his love and know his power. It was so easy to believe then, for it was so obvious that Jesus was with us. He was within us, teaching us, opening the meaning of the scriptures to us. He was working all around us, touching one life after another, opening doors and removing obstacles that we never would have had the faith to tackle on our own. We could have written a book of our own resurrection accounts, just as the evangelists did. We could say we felt him here, we saw him acting there. We were experiencing the presence of the risen Lord.

Yet after those initial days of grace, those intense experiences faded. We began to wonder if it had all been a dream. We no longer sensed the presence of Jesus in our midst as easily or as excitingly as we had at the start. We began to doubt our own memories. Maybe we were wrong. Maybe it had been too much to hope for. Maybe we had made it all up.

Luke recaptures this feeling of the Lord's absence in the ascension narrative. He alone of the four evangelists tries to describe what it must have felt like with the apostles staring off into space, wondering where Jesus had gone (Acts 1:9-11).

At times like that it's natural to pray, and to join with others who are experiencing darkness. And that's what Luke shows the disciples doing. They gather together in the upper room where they had seen him in their midst and felt his love for them. We can easily imagine them going through the same kind of self-doubt that we have sometimes gone through. Was it really him? Maybe we were mistaken. Maybe we wanted him so much that we deluded ourselves. How can we be really sure that it wasn't just our imagination playing tricks on us? They could have easily been asking themselves questions like that as they prayed and waited, hoping for the Lord's return.

The power, it seems, had gone out of their lives, even as it sometimes seems to go out of ours. So they did the only thing that they could do, the only thing that we can do when we no longer feel the Lord's real presence. They prayed and waited, confused yet hoping for something, anything, to happen. In that darkness, they shared the suffering of Jesus on the cross, experiencing the agony with him, yet trusting in the Father for some kind of resurrection, for some kind of light.

They are not disappointed.

The Spirit Transforms

The power comes; not as they expected it, but it comes. The power comes; not as Jesus returning right away in glory, but it comes. It comes in a new way which Luke, searching his imagination for an appropriate image, describes as tongues of fire:

> When the day of Pentecost came, they gathered together in one room. Suddenly they heard a noise like a powerful wind coming out of the sky, which grew till it filled the whole house where they were meeting. Something that seemed like tongues of fire appeared, then separated and came to rest on each of them. They were all filled with the Holy Spirit.
>
> (Acts 2:1-4)

They are transformed. By no effort of their own, they are changed into people of conviction and action. By accepting the gift of the Holy Spirit, they receive power. By opening themselves to whatever God would give them, they permit God to enter into their lives. By letting themselves be emptied of their own security, they allow the Spirit of God to fill them.

To be filled with the Spirit, we must ask for the Spirit. But it is not enough to ask with our lips. We have to empty ourselves of our self-sufficiency if we are to receive the Holy Spirit. We have to empty ourselves of all our idols, if we are to have room for the true God within us. We have to be like the apostles in the upper room, aware of our nothingness, so that God the creator can make something out of nothing.

To experience the Spirit, we must yearn for the Spirit. We must seek it, desire it, long for it. We must make ourselves ready to receive God's gift by asking for it not only with our mind but also with our heart and with our gut. Jesus said, "Ask and you will receive," but if we do not really ask, how can we ever really receive?

When we have done that, all we can do is let God love us, let God give grace to us, let God be gracious to us, let God shower gifts on us. If we wait in patient expectation, the Lord will come. If we do not try to be worthy, the Spirit will be given. If we trust in God's promise, we will not be disappointed.

For some people the baptism of the Spirit is a spiritually drenching experience. They are filled so full so fast that they feel they are going to explode. They are overtaken by the Spirit so dramatically that they know exactly when it happened, even months and years afterward. In some Protestant Churches this is the "normal" experience of conversion. Many in the Catholic charismatic movement have also known this rapid flooding of the Holy Spirit into their hearts. And in the early days of New Jerusalem, many of our young people came to know the Lord in an overwhelming experience of his gracious presence.

For other people, however, the baptism of the Spirit is a gradual immersion which takes place slowly over weeks or months or even years. For them, it's hard to say when they first came to know the Lord. It may even seem there never was a time they did not know him, although they can remember times of special grace when he made his presence unmistakably felt. Or it may be like slowly falling in love with someone you have known for some time, only to discover one day that your friendship has developed into something deeper. In the Catholic Church this has been the more "normal" experience of conversion. It's a reception of the Spirit which happens over time rather than all at once.

Any way it happens is just as real, just as good as any other. The Lord always meets us where we are, and he makes his presence known to us in the way we are most ready to experience it. The Spirit blows where it wills, and though it longs to fill our hearts completely, it will also fill our hearts in whatever measure they are open to the Spirit.

But whatever way it happens, it happens only by our asking, only by our wanting it to happen. God can only fill the emptiness we bring to him. But if we ask the Lord to fill it, we cannot be disappointed. The Spirit cannot withhold itself from any heart that longs to know the powerful presence of God.

When it does happen, we know that we did nothing to deserve it. We realize that it is pure gift. It's so great, we just know we could not have done anything to merit it. There's no explanation possible except God's graciousness. It's a new whole which is greater than the sum of all the parts that go into it. The experience of the Spirit is an undeserved transformation. It's being grabbed by God and lifted into a new relationship.

To be drawn into that relationship is to surrender to the Father, to receive the Spirit, and to know Jesus. It is giving yourself away completely, and receiving back infinitely more than the little that you gave away. This is why surrendering to God does not destroy individuality but actually creates it and empowers it. The highest form of self-possession is the capacity to give yourself away. It is the highest form of freedom; it is the perfect act of freedom.

Jesus was supremely free in the moment of his crucifixion. He took all that was humanly his and gave it away completely to his Father. He took his own and our humanity within the giving of himself in free surrender to the Father's will for him and us. And such was the power of his giving that it gives us the power to give ourselves as he did. It is a received power. It is a gift. It is the power of God.

The Spirit Creates Church

To open ourselves to receive the gift of the Holy Spirit is to enter a new relationship with God. It is a relationship that is known not just with the head but also with the heart and gut. We experience it, we feel it. It is a relationship not just with the Father but also with Jesus and with his Spirit. We know them not just as names but as persons. It is a relationship not just between ourselves and God but between ourselves and everyone else who surrenders to the Father, acknowledges Jesus as Lord, and receives the power of the Holy Spirit. It is the relationship which we call the Church.

All this is contained in Luke's dramatic portrayal of the apostles in the upper room. The Pentecost experience is the beginning of the Church. It is the igniting of the explosion which goes on for chapter after chapter in Acts. Now the apostles know for sure the faithfulness of the Father. Now they know firsthand the power of the Spirit. Now they know with certainty that Jesus is Lord.

Of course we do not see all of this in those few verses about Pentecost (Acts 2:1-4). We see it rather in the changed lives of the apostles. We read about it when time after time the Spirit enables them to do the humanly impossible. The remainder of the book of Acts is a lengthy commentary on those verses.

Right away we begin to hear what the Pentecost experience meant to the early Church in Peter's proclamation to the crowd that gathers near the house in wonderment. He speaks first of the Holy Spirit:

> This is what the prophet Joel was talking about when he said, speaking on behalf of God, "In the days to come, I will pour out my spirit on everyone. Your sons and daughters shall prophesy, those who are young will see visions, and those who are old will dream dreams. When the time comes, I will pour out my spirit even on servants and handmaids, and they will speak in my name. I will display wonders in the heavens and show signs on the earth, even blood and fire and clouds of smoke." (Acts 2:16-19)

Having said this, Peter goes on to speak about Jesus:

> God showed his approval of Jesus of Nazareth by working wonders through him and giving you powerful signs, as you are well aware. It was God's intention to allow you to take this man and—as God knew you would—kill him by turning him over to gentiles for crucifixion. But God freed him from the pangs of death and raised him to life, for the scriptures foretold that death would not be able to hold him down. (Acts 2:22-24)

Peter and the others with him stand before the people of Jerusalem as witnesses. As he says, "This man Jesus was raised up by God, and we are all witnesses to that" (Acts 2:32). He does not give them a philosophical explanation for it. He does not offer them logical proof. He simply says, in effect, "Our lives are proof. Some power has touched us all. How can we explain what has happened to us? All we can say is that we came to trust in Jesus Christ as our Lord, and by the power of the God who raised him up, he has made us a new creation. So we stand before you now, unashamed to be his witnesses. He is the Lord! Believe in him!"

Then, according to Luke (Acts 2:37-41), the second great miracle of Pentecost happens. The crowd which is listening to the word being proclaimed to them receives that word into their hearts, they accept Jesus as their Lord, and their lives too are changed. And it's not a crowd of 30, or 300, but 3,000!

This sounds farfetched, in a way. The best preachers in the world would have a hard time speaking in the open air to so many people, and they would never expect their words to have that kind of total impact. Yet here's this fisherman doing it on his very first try!

But there's a truth to what Luke says. When I preach Jesus and get out of the way so that people can encounter him instead of me, he teaches them. I don't have to teach them. I've done my job as a preacher. Then the Spirit gets to work, speaking a word of comfort to one, of forgiveness to another, of knowledge to a third, of wisdom to a fourth. They meet Jesus in the Spirit, and they don't need me any more. They have already received more than I could ever give to them.

The Spirit is always a gratuitous gift. It's always an unmerited favor. It's always pure grace. Like wind, it cannot be seen. Like smoke, it cannot be controlled. The Spirit is elusive, blowing where it wills. But like fire, the Spirit can be felt. The Spirit is experienced as the warmth of God's love. And like blood, it is experienced as a vitality within. The Spirit is supremely intimate, yet supremely transcendent.

As a transcendent experience, coming to us from beyond ourselves, we enter into a new relationship with the Lord. It is first of all a relationship in prayer, a one-to-one relationship. It's a personal experience of the risen Christ. It's knowing Jesus, talking with him, listening to him, and just being present to one another in the Spirit. That relationship is the basis of authentic Christianity.

Sadly, so many Catholics never experience that relationship. They never know the Lord, even though they have heard a lot about him. They can never say to someone else, "I have been with the Lord. I have heard his voice. I have known his love." So they have nothing that nonbelievers don't have. They have nothing special that others might desire. Their lives as Christians lack power. They are no different from anybody else.

To enter into that relationship, we have to let go of ourselves. We have to surrender control of our lives and let the Spirit be given to us. We think that we might lose our individuality, yet surrendering to God actually increases our individuality. For once in our lives we are truly free to become ourselves rather than what others want us to be. The highest form of self-possession is the capacity to give ourselves away. So by giving ourselves completely to God, we come to be possessed by him and to full possession of ourselves at the same time.

We experience the difference in our lives, and often others see it in us, too. We have something they desire, and yet we know that it is not ours to give. In fact, we do not have it; in a way, it has us. And it is something that they can receive only by giving themselves away, and allowing themselves to be possessed by the Holy Spirit.

Our new relationship with the Lord is not just a one-to-one relationship. It is not just a relationship in the spirit, but a relationship in the flesh as well. It is an incarnate relationship with an incarnate Lord, risen in his body, the Church. It is a new relationship to a new community of others who have also come to know the Lord personally. It is a sharing of a brand new life, a giving and receiving from each other in a very down-to-earth way.

The last verses of the second chapter of Acts gives us a picture of the early Christian community:

All those who trusted in the Lord lived together and owned everything in common. They sold their possessions and divided the proceeds among themselves, giving everyone what they needed. Day after day they went as a body to the temple for worship, but they met in smaller household groups for the breaking of bread. Their meals were simple

and joyful, and they shared their food generously,
praising God. Everyone looked up to them, and the
Lord added daily to the community those who were
being saved. (Acts 2:44-47)

We see here a community of the new disciples of Jesus,
living in the vitality of his Spirit, as children of the Father. They
live as Jesus did, trusting in God's providence and thanking him
for his gifts. Individually and together they live as Jesus did,
sharing all they have been given and laying their lives down for
one another.

The Christian life is meant to be lived in community. It
is not a Jesus-and-me religion. It is a sharing of the Spirit in the
body of Christ. It's a relationship with the Lord that is discovered
and nurtured in relationship with other people. Through their
love and care and faithfulness to us, we experience the love and
care and faithfulness of Christ. And through our acceptance and
concern and service to them, we incarnate Christ's forgiveness
and healing and salvation. We make Christ real in the world by
living in his Spirit in relation to one another.

But the new life of the Christian community is not
supposed to remain in the Church, any more than Christ kept
his own life to himself. It is meant to be shared, to be given
away just as freely as it has been received. The rest of the book
of Acts recounts literally the "acts of the apostles," that is, the
activities of those who went out from the community to bring
the life of Christ to others.

Right away, at the beginning of chapter 3, Luke gives us
the first of many examples of the Church's apostolic activity. As
Peter and John are going to the temple for afternoon worship,
a crippled beggar at the gate asks them for a handout. They stop
at his plea, and look at him:

Then Peter said, "I don't have any money, but what
I do have I'll give you. In the name of the messiah,
Jesus of Nazareth, walk!" Then Peter took him by the
hand and pulled him up. Immediately the crippled
man's feet and ankles became strong. He jumped up
and stood for a moment, and then began to walk

around. He went with them into the temple, walking, jumping about, and praising God. When people heard him and saw what he was doing, they recognized him as the cripple who used to sit begging at the Beautiful Gate. They were struck with amazement, and unable to explain what had happened to him. (Acts 3:6-10)

The poor and the lame of the world still turn to Christians and look at us expectantly, as the beggar looked at Peter and John. They hope to get something from us. But what do we so often say to them? We say, "Come, join our parish. We have plenty of money, even a credit union. The St. Vincent de Paul Society will help you out, too, if you need it. We have a parish council, and we're very democratic. We have nice liturgies, even a guitar mass if you want. We have a good Catholic school, or if you prefer, you can send your children to our CCD program."

Today more than ever we must do as Peter did on that first Pentecost afternoon. We must preach Jesus first, not the Church. We must have the courage to stand before others and say he is our Lord, he is the reason our lives are transformed. We must stand on the power of the Spirit, rejoicing in what God has done in our lives, praising and thanking him, and eager to share the life of the Spirit with others.

If we do that, Church will happen. Communities will be formed. Liturgies of thanksgiving and praise will erupt. People will be free to question their habits of individualism and self-protection. There will be sharing of goods and healing of lives and forgiveness of sins. We will stop creating enemies. For God will be in our midst, as he is in every body of Christ which is energized by the Spirit.

If we do that, the poor of the world will be rich beyond measure. Impoverished lives will be filled with new meaning. If we do that, the lame in our society will rise up and walk. Lives that limp along on handouts from day to day will jump with joy to the amazement of others.

In the end, it is not our own doing, or grace would not be grace. It is God's gift, not a reward for work well done. It is nothing for us to be boastful about. We are God's work of art, created in Christ Jesus. All we can do is be what God's Spirit makes us to be, and be thankful to God for the riches he has bestowed on us. Humility, gratitude and loving service to others are probably the most appropriate responses we can make.

CHAPTER FOUR

Mary, Prayer and the Church:
Let It Be!

We realize today that God is neither masculine nor feminine. In the scriptures, however, God is always spoken of as masculine. Yahweh is a warrior and king in much of the Old Testament. The God of the New Testament is addressed as "our Father." Yet Yahweh also exhibits many traditionally feminine traits: gentle love, patient endurance, tender mercy, strong feeling, willing forgiveness. And the God of Jesus is in many respects motherly. The androgyny of the biblical image of God is that of a male figure with female attributes.

Humankind, created in God's image, is also both masculine and feminine. Not too long ago, however, it was common to refer to the human race as "mankind" and to speak of "God and man" to refer to the relation between the divine and the human. In terms of the language that we used, it was a very masculine relationship. The very ways we spoke of divinity and humanity prevented us from realizing that the scriptures see humankind in front of God as radically feminine.

Humanity as Radically Feminine

Biblically speaking, God is the giver and creation is the receiver. In the first account of creation, God gives order to the formless chaos which receives the forms of nature that make the world good. In the second chapter of Genesis, God gives life to a lifeless earth, again bringing into being all good things, including man and woman. We sometimes speak of "mother earth" and "mother nature," a reminder of how even nonbiblical religions recognized the need for impregnation by a "father god" to create the miracle of life.

Likewise in our own religious experience, we know that we are all feminine before the Lord. The moment of conversion is a surrender to a greater power which plants the seed of spiritual life in us. And as we walk the journey of faith, we are constantly dependent on God's strength and guidance, the way that woman has always stereotypically depended on man.

Thus, the image of the human race in relation to God has often been one of femininity. In the erotic imagery of the Song of Songs, early Christian writers saw the Church being courted and seduced by the Lord, her lover. In the writings of the prophets, Israel is portrayed as the harlot who is loved by her faithful spouse, Yahweh, despite her running off to worship other gods. In the psalms, God is usually described as masculinely mighty, while the psalmist or the people are shown to be in feminine dependence on his strength. These attributes that we call masculine and feminine are often culturally determined, but they are one way in which people in the past have tried to articulate the profound mystery of all that God is in relation to humanity.

At the beginning of the Old Testament we see Eve, the mother of the human race, the womb from which all humanity will be born. After the fall she is naked and helpless, totally dependent on the mercy of God. But Yahweh does not leave her without hope. In what has sometimes been called the first announcement of the good news, Yahweh looks at the serpent who has tempted Eve and says to it:

> I will put emnity between you and the woman,
> between your seed and her seed. You will strike out
> at her offspring's heel, but he will strike your head.
> (Genesis 3:15)

God promises that even though human beings will always have to struggle against evil, in the end the human will triumph over the satanic. Through all the bitterness of history, God will unite with the human effort and give it the strength it needs to conquer the demonic forces in the world.

At the beginning of the New Testament we meet Mary, who gives birth to the one who will perfectly fulfill the prophecy of Genesis. She is perfectly receptive to the word which comes to her, and that word of God is the seed which becomes the Son of God, the supreme gift of the Father to a needy and helpless humanity.

Then, at the end of the scriptures, Mary appears again in the Book of Revelation. The woman of the apocalypse bears a male child who is destined to rule the world from the throne of God. The devil follows her into the desert and tries to devour her, taking the appearance of a dragon who wages war on all her children (Revelation 12:1-17). But, in the end, her Son and children triumph, having been given the victory by God.

Mary's role as woman—and therefore as humankind before the Lord—is emphasized in John's gospel when the evangelist refers to her not by name but by title. When he has Jesus address her as "woman" at the wedding feast at Cana, John is symbolizing that she is not just Mary but also our own corporate identity before the Lord. She comes to Jesus asking, for only he can give. At first he does not seem to hear her, but she is confident that Jesus will provide what is needed. We know this from the way she immediately directs the servants to do whatever her son commands (John 2:5).

The six large stone jars in the story are receptive and, in that sense, also symbols of the feminine. The water which the servants pour into them symbolizes life which lacks the vitality needed for feasting. We can imagine Mary pleading for humanity to be filled with something more than sterile life, to be filled with the Spirit which only the Lord can give.

And the Lord does not disappoint her. In response to her request, he lavishly pours out 150 gallons of the very best wine for the assembled guests. It is a wonderful symbol of the fullness of the Spirit, the inebriating wine of salvation which transforms everyday life into a party. But the Lord cannot give new life until humanity, eternally feminine, comes and asks for it.

At the end of John's gospel we see Mary again, this time

standing at the foot of the cross. Again Jesus addresses her as "woman," showing that *in her* all humanity must come to Calvary to be with the Lord in his crucifixion. Just as she suffers in the absurdity of her situation, we too must suffer in the face of the apparent triumph of evil. In and through Mary, we all stand at the cross. The crucifixion image is not whole or inviting unless we are there with him—in her.

Mary in Luke's Gospel

Of all the books in the New Testament, the Gospel According to Luke gives the fullest account of Mary both as mother of Jesus and as symbol of humanity. She is a real mother and completely human. No plaster statue or artist's madonna, she is a Jewish girl who grows to womanhood in the company of a son who is as much a mystery to her as a child can be. That's very real, as any mother today can testify. And yet she is a woman of extraordinary faith, which is what sets her apart and makes her a model for the rest of us. Even though she does not fully understand what God is asking of her, she believes with all her heart that it can and will be done, and she acts accordingly.

Although Luke does not give us a glorified and unrealistic portrait of Mary, neither does he give us an undoctored photograph. Remember that the gospels are not newspaper reports but faith documents, attesting to the beliefs of the first-century Church. What we read in the first three chapters of his gospel, therefore, is not so much a historical account as a theological account. It is filled with allusions to Genesis and Exodus, Judith and Ruth, Isaiah and Daniel, Psalms and many others books in the Old Testament. In so doing Luke not only situates his work in relation to the whole of scripture, but he also gives it a larger significance. He is speaking not only about individuals but about exemplary individuals. He is not so much describing particular events as much as he is portraying the universal meaning of those events.

As we begin to examine the events in Mary's life at the beginning of Luke's gospel, therefore, we must see Mary not only as a person but also as an exemplar for all persons. She is a particular woman, but she is also a model of faith for all women and men. And the events which Luke describes are not simply events in one woman's life; they portray the eternal meaning of every life of faith.

Annunciation

The first event is the annunciation, when Mary is told that she is to be the mother of the messiah. The many artists who have depicted this event have made it a familiar scene, with the angel greeting the woman who is not yet sure why this is happening to her:

> "Rejoice, you who are full of God's favor! The Lord is with you. Blessed are you among women." She was deeply troubled by his words, and she wondered what this greeting might mean. (Luke 1:28-29)

The angel greets Mary with the word *rejoice* for it is always good news when the Lord speaks to us. Yet so often we cannot be sure right away whether we are hearing something from God or just from our own imagination. Thus the woman wonders and listens further:

> But the angel went on to say to her, "Do not be afraid, Mary. God has favored you." (Luke 1:30)

God is calling her to the way of faith, which is not a way of fear. When the Lord is present, there is no need to fear. When the Lord calls, the only need is to trust. The woman is not to doubt God's favor, the gift of God's love. The word in Greek for "favor" is *charis*, which is also translated "grace." For Mary, then, this is a grace experience. Like every person's experience of grace, hers is one of favor and acceptance by God.

Each of us has our own calling from God, what God asks us alone to do. The call comes personally and individually. It speaks to where we are and to what we are capable of. And so Mary hears the angel telling what the Lord is asking of her in this moment:

"You are to conceive and bear a son, and give him
the name Jesus. He will be great, and he will be called
Son of the Most High. The Lord God will give him
the throne of David, his forefather. He will rule over
the house of Jacob forever, and his reign will have no
end." (Luke 1:31-33)

The woman listens. Again she wonders. How is this
possible? She seeks discernment. She questions:

Then Mary said to the angel, "How can this be, since
I am a virgin?" (Luke 1:34)

The meaning here is twofold. On the first level Mary is
asking the obvious, since she has not had sexual relations with
her betrothed husband. But at a second level, she is speaking
for all of us. The biblical meaning of virginity is not just physical
intactness. It is symbolic of spiritual emptiness. Unless the Lord
plants a seed in us, we can bear no fruit. Unless we allow God
to come into us and give us the Spirit, we are spiritually barren.
And so the angel explains to the woman how her barrenness
will be overcome:

"The Holy Spirit will come upon you, and the power
of the Most High will overshadow you," the angel
answered. "For this reason, the holy child will be
called Son of God. Not only that, but your relative
Elizabeth has conceived a son, despite her age. People
thought she was sterile, but she is already into the
sixth month of her pregnancy. Nothing is impossible
for God!" (Luke 1:35-37)

Through Mary, Luke is opening up a new realm of
possibility for us. He is saying to his readers that the way of
faith is the way of unheard-of possibilities. The power of the
Spirit is such that even the impossible is possible. Even the
undreamt-of can be dreamed, and those dreams can become
real. But it does not happen to everyone. It does not happen
automatically. It happens only to those who put their whole

104

trust in the Lord. So Luke continues:

> Mary said, "I am the handmaid of the Lord. Let it be
> done to me as you say." (Luke 1:38)

With those words Mary sums up the faith of Abraham
following Yahweh's call across the desert, the faith of Moses
kneeling before the burning bush, the faith of the prophets
listening to the word which came to them, the faith of Job
standing in the midst of the whirlwind. She says, in effect, "I
am human, but the Lord is God. I am the Lord's servant, and
he is the master. I don't know how this will happen. I don't
completely understand what this will mean. But I know that the
word of the Lord does not lie. So let it be! Let it happen! I am
in God's hands, and I know he will not fail me."

Mary responds to God in an attitude of listening to the
really real. She attunes herself to the word which is coming to
her, and she trusts that it is speaking truth to her. By
participating in that dialogue with reality, she allows the truth
which is spoken to become real. She does not hide from the
truth; she faces it. She does not run from the truth; she embraces
it. She sees the truth of what is, and in doing so, she lets it be.

Mary is therefore the model of prayer for all Christians.
Prayer is getting in touch with reality, letting it speak to us, and
incarnating the word which comes to us. We let it happen; we
don't make it happen. For saying yes to God in prayer does not
just mean acknowledging that we heard it. It means changing
our lives in accordance with that word. It means engaging that
word with our whole being and letting it alter our existence. For
prayer is a dialogue between life and life, between divine life
and human life, between the life of the Spirit and the life of the
flesh. Unless we enflesh the word of God and let it become
incarnate in us, it cannot become real in the world.*

---

*This notion of incarnational faith is explained more fully in *The Great
Themes of Scripture: Old Testament*, pp. 125-130.

105

Visitation

When she receives this word of the Lord, therefore, the woman does not turn in upon herself. Rather she goes out toward others. And so Mary walks to visit Elizabeth, whom the angel had said was six months pregnant. As they meet, her aging relative echoes the words of the angel:

> Blessed are you of all women, and blessed is the fruit of your womb!...Blessed are you, for you trusted that the Lord's word to you would be fulfilled.
>
> (Luke 1:42, 45)

So Luke, through the words of Elizabeth, reaffirms that the greatest blessing of the person of faith is to know that the word of God has been planted and to trust that it will come to fruition. The "poor of Yahweh" (the *anawim* in Hebrew) have always known this. They are the ones who suffered in slavery in Egypt, waiting for the Lord's deliverance. They are the ones who endured bondage in Babylonia, comforted by the prophets in exile with them. They are the ones who waited centuries for the messiah, hoping to be liberated from foreign domination. They are the ones who, even today, having no power of their own, are totally dependent on the power of God.

The glory of the *anawim* is their salvation by God. Their greatest blessing is not what they accomplish but what God does for them. For Luke, Mary is the exemplary "poor one" of Yahweh, for what has been accomplished in her is far beyond her ability. And so, after the angel has said it, after Elizabeth has said it, Mary too proclaims how blessed she is:

> My soul proclaims the greatness of the Lord
> and my spirit exults in God my Savior;
> because he has looked upon the humiliation of his
> servant.
> Yes, from this day onwards all generations will call
> me blessed,
> for the Almighty has done great things for me.
>
> (Luke 1:46b-49a NJB)

106

In Mary's hymn of praise,* Luke sums up the combined wisdom of the Old Testament and the New Testament alike. Some call it the most succinct and perfect summary of biblical spirituality. The moral development of Israel leads up to this, and the spiritual growth of the Church takes off from this. It is the fundamental attitude of every Christian, of every true disciple of Jesus, of every person who trusts in God so totally that God's word can become incarnate in the world.

But this way of the Lord, this total surrender to the Spirit, is a way of suffering. Jesus knew this and he lived it to the utmost. In the gospels Jesus tries to explain it to his disciples over and over again, even though they do not fully comprehend it until after his resurrection. Here at the beginning of Luke's gospel, the evangelist speaks the same word to every disciple by having it spoken to Mary, the perfect disciple.

Presentation in the Temple

After the birth of Jesus, Mary and Joseph bring Jesus to the temple for the Jewish rite of circumcision. There they meet the prophet Simeon, who takes the child into his arms and says to his mother:

> You see this child? He is destined to be the undoing
> of many in Israel, and the uplifting of many others.
> He will be a sign that is rejected, and the secret
> thoughts of many hearts will be exposed. And you—a
> sword will pierce your own soul as well. (Luke 2:34-35)

Soon after this Luke gives us a vignette which illustrates what Simeon was saying to Mary. The scene is 12 years later, when Jesus has reached the age of adult responsibility according to the Jewish understanding of maturity. It is the age at which a Jewish child today becomes *Bar* (or *Bat*) *Mitzvah*, a Son (or Daughter) of the Commandment. The family goes to Jerusalem for the feast of Passover, but during the journey home the parents of Jesus discover that their son is not in their caravan.

---

* See also *The Great Themes of Scripture: Old Testament*, pp. 129-130.

They return to Jerusalem where they discover him in the temple, discussing the scriptures with the teachers of the Law. Of course they are both distraught, and Mary says to her son:

> "My child, why have you done this to us? Look how worried your father and I have been! We've been searching all over for you!" Jesus replied, "Why were you searching for me? Didn't you realize that I have to do the work which my Father has given me?" But they did not understand what he meant.
>
> (Luke 2:48-50)

At this point, then, Mary does not understand. She has given herself completely to God, even without understanding all that would mean. She doesn't understand, yet she is willing to "stand under" the mystery and the mercy of God. She is a woman of faith—not the woman of knowledge Eve had wanted to be. She is the model of faith for every woman and man who believes the Lord's word can be trusted. She is willing to outstare the darkness, however long it lasts. And so, Luke adds:

> He returned to Nazareth with them, and was obedient to them. His mother kept all these things in her heart. And Jesus matured into manhood, growing in wisdom, and loved by God and people alike.
>
> (Luke 2:51-52)

Mary, Model of Discipleship

Except for one further glimpse of Mary in Luke's gospel, we do not see her again until she is with the other disciples at Pentecost in the Book of Acts. Luke's next-to-last word about her is that she ponders all that has happened and waits for the promise of the Lord to be fulfilled. She does not understand the meaning of this son of hers. Yet she never doubts that somehow, in some way, she will see the fulfillment of the word she has been given. But what that itself means she is unsure—and she is willing to be unsure. She has given over control. She makes no claims on reality or God or others.

108

For the next 18 years, Mary's life was uneventful. It must have been quite an ordinary life. The life of the disciple is often very ordinary, even when it is a life of extraordinary faith. Perhaps she even thought at some point that if this child of hers was something special, he ought to do something special. But still she waited. She waited through the 15th year, and the 20th year, and the 25th year, until the 30th year of Jesus' maturity. She waited on the Lord's timing. She waited for the hour that was to come. She did not try to force it. She trusted that what God wanted to happen would happen. She needed only to be faithful, for she knew that God is faithful.

Discipleship is often like that. We do everything we think the Lord is calling us to do, but nothing happens. We pray and read the scriptures, but we do not feel any holier or any smarter. We get involved in our parish or our prayer group, but they do not seem to get any better from one year to the next. We work for justice in our neighborhood, or for peace in the world, but things seem to stay pretty much as they have always been.

Luke's reminder to all disciples, spoken through his silence about Mary, is this: Waiting in the silence is sometimes precisely what God is asking of us. God needs us to do God's work, but in the end, the work is God's. God will bring it to fruition, not us.

And yet all the while we wait, something is happening. All the while the Spirit is working. In Luke's gospel this is symbolized by Jesus growing slowly into manhood, waiting on the Father's timing for the proper hour to begin the work he has been called to do.

Finally, the time arrives. When Jesus is about 30, he is baptized by John in the Jordan, and he receives the anointing by the Spirit which launches him into his public ministry. He preaches the word which has been given to him, but as Simeon had foretold, he is accepted by some but rejected by many. He does not become a great and glorious figure. To most, he looks like just another country preacher.

Why, through all those months and years, does this woman still believe? Humanly speaking, nothing much seems to be happening. Most of those who go to see Jesus are just spectators. They've heard that this country preacher is a little different from the others. Sometimes he does amazing things, like healing people and casting out demons. But they do not really listen to what he is saying. They only go to look, wanting to see a miracle.

Sometimes Jesus even draws large crowds. Luke's last mention of Mary is just such an occasion:

> His mother and his brothers came looking for him,
> but they could not get to him because of the crowd.
> He was told, "Your mother and brothers are standing
> outside and want to see you." But he said in answer,
> "My mother and my brothers are those who hear the
> word of God and put it into practice."
> (Luke 8:19-21 NJB)

In Matthew's and Mark's treatment of this scene, Jesus contrasts his family with the hearers of the word. In Luke's interpretation, on the other hand, Jesus affirms that his mother and brothers are disciples, that is, they hear God's word and practice it. And this fits in perfectly with Luke's picture of the earliest Christian community: the 11 apostles (minus Judas), several women, Mary and other relatives of Jesus (Acts 1:14). Of all these disciples, Mary is the first and foremost. For 30 years she said her yes to the word of the Lord, long before the others even heard it. She was the first to incarnate that word and bring it forth into the world. And now she is not alone but a member of the community of faith gathered in the upper room. She is thus the prototype of the true disciple.

Mary is also the foremost among the disciples because she endured everything that any disciple could be called by God to endure for the sake of the kingdom. Day after day she said her yes to the Lord, even though she did not know where she was being led. She was led to the meaninglessness of her son's crucifixion, the absurdity of seeing him murdered by the very people she respected. Yet her faith did not falter and so, three days later, she witnessed his resurrection as well.

Mary has seen it all, from before the beginning until after the end. She is the unique witness to the whole life of Christ in the world, from before its conception in her until its

110

transformation and continuation in the Church. She is the ultimate disciple, giving birth not only to the Christ but also to the Church by being at the center of the earliest community.

Virgin and Mother

In the Catholic tradition, Mary has been called the mother of the Church as well as the mother of Christ. Obviously she was not the actual mother of everyone in the early community. But, because of her attitude of total trust and commitment to God, which preceded and exemplified the trust and commitment of the early community, she was the spiritual mother of all the disciples. It was her initial reception of the Spirit which foreshadowed the reception of the Spirit at Pentecost. And it was her giving birth to Jesus which was the model for the incarnation of Christ in the early Church.

Besides being mother, though, Mary is also virgin. The Church has no earthly father. The Father of the Church is the Father of our Lord, the *Abba* to whom Jesus prayed and in whom he put his total trust. The Spirit of the Church is the Spirit of the Father, who fills the Church with courage and conviction, care and commitment. The Spirit overshadows the disciples at Pentecost and pours itself into them, making them the new body of Christ in the world.

In relation to the birth of Jesus, Mary has likewise been called virgin as well as mother. Sometimes in Christian history this has been taken to mean mere physical virginity, especially in periods when the biblical meaning of virginity was not understood. But properly to understand Mary's virginity in relation to Jesus, we have to understand the meaning of virginity in the scriptures. By understanding biblical virginity we can then come to a renewed appreciation of the spiritual virginity of every person before God. In the same way, by understanding biblical motherhood we can more deeply appreciate the motherhood of every Christian—and of the Church itself.

To begin with, we must understand that the Israelites had no great appreciation of physical virginity, except that it was the proper condition of a young unmarried woman. A Jewish girl

111

was expected to marry at a fairly early age, usually by the arrangement of her family, and after that she looked forward to being a mother. A happy woman was one who was married to a loving husband and who was blessed with many children.

A married woman who could not bear children was the unhappiest of women. She was barren, unfruitful, unfulfilled. She was, as it were, a virgin beyond her time. She was incapable of bringing forth life and, in that sense, no better off than a virgin. Empty and receptive, she was in a state of total dependence on forces outside herself.

A mother, by contrast, was a fulfilled and blessed woman. Her fruitfulness was her gift from God, her special grace. His favor was demonstrated in her children, in the new life which poured forth from her. If woman needed the blessing of God to fill her empty virginity, it was almost as though God needed the virginity of woman to show his creative power. His grace could overcome the emptiness which the power of man alone was impotent to fill with life.

The Bible contains many stories of woman's barrenness being turned to fruitfulness by the power of God. In chapter 17 of Genesis, Sarah is both sterile and past the age for childbearing, but she receives the word of God that she will have a son, and Isaac is born of that promise. In chapter 25 Rebecca is barren until Yahweh answers the prayer of her husband, and through Yahweh's power she gives birth to twins, Esau and Jacob. Then again in chapter 30 we see Rachel who is childless despite her strong desire for a son, until God fills her emptiness and she gives birth to Joseph.

In the First Book of Samuel we see the same pattern repeated. Hannah pleads with Yahweh to take away her shame and give her a son. One day a temple priest hears her prayer and assures her that it will be answered. Confidently she goes to her husband's bed that night and conceives the child who grows up to be the prophet Samuel. Hannah's prayer of thanksgiving in chapter 2 is very similar to Mary's Magnificat in Luke's gospel. She is, so to speak, the spiritual ancestor of Mary, which is perhaps why Christian tradition came to identify Mary's mother as Anna.

Even in the New Testament we find this theme of God

filling the emptiness of the receptive woman with life. At the beginning of Luke's gospel, Mary's relative Elizabeth is like Sarah, barren and beyond the years for bearing children. Like Hannah, too, Elizabeth is the wife of a pious man who goes to the temple to offer sacrifice. Then, like both Sarah and Hannah, Elizabeth's faithful waiting is at long last answered, and she gives birth to the prophet who announces the coming of the messiah, John the Bapist.

For Luke, as we have seen, Mary is the woman who sums up and goes beyond all of her scriptural predecessors. She is completely dependent upon God for her fruitfulness. She is completely open to receiving him, and her total receptivity is answered by God's Word coming to her and incarnating itself in her womb. She who is completely virgin becomes completely mother. The themes of biblical virginity and biblical motherhood are united in Mary.

On the other hand, the biblical theme of fall from grace and loss of God's favor is turned upside down. The son to whom Mary gives birth is completely Son of God. Jesus is the beginning of a new humanity. After Eve's no to God, she becomes the mother of all of sinful humanity. But after Mary's yes to God, *she* becomes the mother of all of redeemed humanity. The biblical fall is reversed: With Jesus, all humanity will be raised up, for all will share in his resurrection.

Throughout the scriptures, as we have seen, the virgin and the barren woman are symbolic of human impotence to bring forth life of its own volition. They are images of human powerlessness to give birth to any goodness without God. Yet when the biblical woman turns to God expectantly, desiring to do his will, receptive to the seed that he will plant in her, her emptiness is filled. She receives the power to do what she cannot do on her own, and she becomes mother.

Mary therefore is the symbol of how human barrenness is made fruitful by being receptive to the word of God. She is the image of all those who wait upon God's timing, always with that faith which is the sign of God's favor. She does not fall from grace but is lifted up from her lowliness to be exalted by the power of God. The Catholic doctrine of Mary's assumption is a theological reflection of this biblical image. For all Christians this image is reflected in the doctrine of the resurrection of the body, the teaching that all will rise as Christ did, fully human and fully alive.

There is yet another symbolic theme in the Bible which harmonizes with the theme of the virgin who becomes mother through the power of God. It is the theme of the poor ones, the *anawim*, the little ones of God who wait expectantly for God's deliverance. Especially during the exile in Babylonia, the prophets sounded this theme in speaking to the remnant of Israel hoping to return some day to Palestine.

The prophet Zephaniah addresses the exiles as "the daughter of Jerusalem" and "the daughter of Zion" (the hill on which the city rests). The image of daughter is feminine and virginal, for the lowly ones in exile are powerless and empty:

> Daughter of Zion, shout for joy!
> Israel, shout out loud!
> Daughter of Jerusalem,
> rejoice and be glad with all your heart!
> The Lord has repealed your sentence,
> and he has driven your enemies away.
> You have nothing more to fear:
> for Yahweh, the king of Israel, is in your midst.
>
> (Zephaniah 3:14-15)

The phrase in Hebrew translated here as "in your midst" is the same as the one translated in other places as "in your womb." The image is that of a woman who carries the savior of Israel within her. She is the embodiment of the "humble and lowly people" who "seek refuge in the name of Yahweh" (Zephaniah 3:12).

In the Christian tradition, it was Mary who came to be addressed as "the daughter of Zion" and "the daughter of Jerusalem." She was seen not only as bearing the Savior within her but also as being at one with the *anawim*. She is the perfect example of the perfect Israelite, the humble poor one who lives in complete dependence on the Lord. These are the lowly ones whom Jesus says know the secret of the kingdom: that it is in their midst, that it is within them—in their womb. It is they who give birth to the Church. It is they who bring Christ into the world. For this reason, Mary is not only the mother of Christ, she is also a model of the Church.

The Femininity of the Church

In the past, Catholics have spoken of *Sancta Mater Ecclesia*, Holy Mother Church, and in many ways the Church was like a mother to us. In the days before modern transportation, many of us grew up knowing only other Catholics. In the days before contemporary education, many of us believed that the only Christian teaching was Catholic doctrine. In the days before the Holy Spirit opened our hearts to the beauty of the scriptures, many of us depended entirely on the truth of the Catholic magisterium. Being a Catholic was a womb to tomb experience, and the Church was a great mother who gave us spiritual and intellectual and even cultural life.

And yet the Church of the past, despite its so-called motherhood, was often very masculine. The hierarchy was composed entirely of men. The administration of the Church was very bureaucratic, even autocratic. The magisterium of the Church was at best fatherly and at worst paternalistic. Because of this the femininity of the Church was often not felt by Catholics or perceived by non-Catholics.

The people in the Middle Ages had a more Marian sense of the Church's femininity. Medieval artists sometimes portrayed Mary as a woman wearing a giant cope. Beneath the cope were all the people of the Church, rich and poor alike, pictured like little ones clinging to and identifying with their mother. They were, and wanted to be, like her. She was, and would always be, one of them. Together they were united in their attitude of dependence on and trust in God. Together they were feminine before the Lord.

This medieval image is closer to the biblical image of humanity as virginal—that is, barren—without God and fruitful only when it allows the Lord to fill its need. It is also closer to the scriptural image of Mary as the eternal woman, eternally virgin in her emptiness, yet eternally mother in the fullness

115

which God has given her. It allows us to see that if Mary is a model of the Church, as the Second Vatican Council has declared her to be, then the Church must be virgin as well as mother.

The masculinity and paternalism mentioned above result when the Church tries to be mother without also being virgin. It plays the game of Mother Knows Best, forgetting that there can be a negative and manipulative side to mothering. It asserts its motherhood in an authoritarian manner and often keeps the children weak and dependent. In doing so, it forgets its own virginity, its need to wait upon the Lord, to be a humble handmaid; it forgets its own call to serve the larger world and not just itself.

Mary was chosen to bring Christ into the world because, in the angel's words, she found favor with God. Or, as the older translation puts it, she was "full of grace." But her grace was her virginity, her emptiness and her willingness to admit her need. She found favor with God because she admitted her nothingness before God's everything. She knew that she was not the savior, and that only God could do all the saving that needed to be done in her and in the world.

That very acknowledgment was Mary's glory. Like the moon, she knew she had no light to give except what she received from the sun. Hers was and is a reflective glory, radiating God's light on a darkened world. But if Mary is a model of the Church, then the Church's glory is likewise in its virginity. By acknowledging its dependence on God, the Church then also becomes mother by allowing the Lord to fill it with his Spirit so that it can bear Christ into the world. It is by being obedient to the Father, and by being receptive to the Word and the Spirit, that the Church finds favor with God, just as Mary did.

Mary is not only a model for the social reality of the Church; she is also a model for the individual reality of every human life. Mary's relationship to God is one of dependence and gratuity: dependence on the Lord for everything she needs; and gratuity from the Lord in everything she receives. If Mary is our model, then we too must always acknowledge our emptiness and allow the Lord to fill us. The scriptures promise that if we do this, as she did, we will not be disappointed. God will always fill us with much more than we give up.

116

It is important to understand this point in the way the Bible teaches it. Too often Catholic spirituality has promoted self-denial and self-abasement in an almost masochistic fashion. We were led to believe by some spiritual writers of the past that putting ourselves down was an end in itself. It was almost as though giving things up and denying our rights was all that was expected of us, and that God was satisfied with that.

That type of Christian spirituality, however, is only half of the biblical spirituality, only the first part of an authentic Marian spirituality. The second part is listening attentively to God's word, saying our yes to it when it comes, and allowing ourselves to be filled with the Spirit so that we can bring Christ into the world. This second step is essential to what we have already called incarnational faith.

Biblical faith and biblical spirituality are one and the same thing: It is a spirituality of fidelity, a faithful trusting in the Lord. This is why we can say that Mary is the exemplar of biblical faith: Her faith is what the whole Old Testament was leading up to, what the whole New Testament is about. Marian spirituality is a faith which allows God to become incarnate in our lives.

A spirituality of pure self-denial is not only half-biblical; it is also half-human. It is a type of Christianity which many people today are repelled by because it seems to say that God wants them to be less than they can be. For this very same reason even sincere Catholics often do not understand the call to self-denial sounded during Lent and Advent. Self-denial for its own sake seems unrewarding, unfulfilling and, therefore, unintelligible.

Biblical faith and Marian spirituality, however, move beyond self-denial to the affirmation of God and the reception of Christ into our lives. Once Mary says her yes to God, God fills her with more than she ever could have expected. She does more than she could ever have dreamed of doing on her own. The reversal which takes place is the one which Isaiah prophesied centuries before:

Sing for joy, you barren woman who did not have
    any children!

Break into songs of gladness, you who did not know
  childbirth!
For the abandoned wife has even more children
than the woman whose husband never left her, says
  the Lord. (Isaiah 54:1)

God turns around our human way of thinking. We think
we have to do it all, but God wants to do it all in us. He wants
to do more in us than we could ever do for ourselves, but in
order for God to do that, we must first acknowledge our own
emptiness. That's really a better way of saying it than speaking
of emptying ourselves. It's not so much that we empty ourselves
out, but that we look within ourselves and admit that everything
we have is gift. It's not so much a matter of self-denial as a
matter of affirming that we are nothing but what has been given
to us. Once we do that, we are free from clinging to what we
have, free to remain unattached to ourselves in any form. Once
we do that, we can let go of the little that we think is ours in
order to receive the riches that God wants to give to us.

This is a wisdom which is hard to understand. It is
especially hard for those of us who have been raised on the ethic
of success and accomplishment. But it is a very biblical wisdom.
The psalmist says:

Unless the Lord builds the house,
the builders' work is useless.
Unless the Lord protects the city,
the sentries' vigilance is futile.
Why do you get up so early,
and then stay up so late,
working so hard for a living?
The Lord provides for those he loves
even during their sleep. (Psalm 127:1-2)

"Don't just do something; stand there!" That's a very
different kind of wisdom from what we are used to. It is the
wisdom of spiritual faith. It is the wisdom of Marian spirituality.
It is a wisdom you can read about in a book, but you cannot
obtain it by reading about it. It is a wisdom which only the Lord

can give, and which can only be received in prayer.

The Femininity of Prayer

In the Gospel According to Luke, we meet another Mary. Like the mother of Jesus and all the women in Luke's gospel, she is a model of that receptive attitude which we all need to bring before the Lord. She is a model of prayer.

In this story of Mary and her sister Martha, the evangelist contrasts those who do their thing for God with those who let God do God's thing for them:

> In the course of their journey [Jesus] came to a village, and a woman named Martha welcomed him into her house. She had a sister called Mary, who sat down at the Lord's feet and listened to him speaking. Now Martha, who was distracted with all the serving, came to him and said, "Lord do you not care that my sister is leaving me to do the serving all by myself? Please tell her to help me." But the Lord answered: "Martha, Martha," he said "you worry and fret about so many things, and yet few are needed, indeed only one. It is Mary who has chosen the better part, and it is not to be taken from her." (Luke 10:38-42 NJB)

Like Martha, we are all tempted to be fussbudgets for the Lord. We are always thinking about doing something for God. Yet Luke makes it clear that Mary is the one who is in the right relationship to Jesus. Outwardly she looks so useless, so impractical, so uninvolved with all that demands to be done. Yet she is the one who is doing what is ultimately the most useful and practical, for she is completely involved in relating to Jesus and listening to him.

That presence and listening to the Lord is the essence of prayer. Prayer is a dialogue between two hearts, the human and the divine. It is a dialogue which is sometimes spoken but just as often unspoken, like the give and take of a close relationship. To be a woman or a man of prayer is to be always in a dialogue.

If we fall out of that relationship of giving and receiving, we are no longer persons of prayer.

That relationship is a form of being in love. When we deeply love someone, we do not have to use words to communicate. The union of our hearts enables us to communicate at a deeper level where the communication becomes communion. We are simply happy to be near the one we love, for then we feel the energy of love flowing between us. The energy we experience in prayer is very much the same. The power we receive in prayer is the love we open ourselves up to when we wait upon the Lord and let him love us.

Being in love comes from falling in love. If you've ever been in love, you know you didn't do it. Somehow when you weren't trying, it just happened. It's a little like the first time you learn to swim. The instructor tells you to lie still and float, but instead you thrash about and sink. Finally you learn to relax and, quite surprisingly, you are buoyed to the top. The water supports you, but only if you are quiet and do nothing. Falling in love is like that, and so is "falling in prayer." It is something you cannot do, but it will happen if you stop your busyness and let yourself fall into it.

Floating is a sort of dialogue between ourselves and the water. By remaining quiet, we tell the water that we trust it, and we allow it to tell us that it will support us. Prayer is that same sort of trust relationship between ourselves and God. If we stop trying to control our own lives, we can experience the power of the Lord supporting us. Very often our prayer is like that, especially after the Lord has told us, "Okay, now that you know who is supporting you, I want you to start swimming." Stroke after stroke we know the Lord is with us, even though we've started moving again.

Sometimes, though, we just float. Sometimes we just let ourselves be still, and we experience in prayer the love which is supporting us. Or to return to the metaphor of being in communion with someone we love, it is like looking into our beloved's eyes and resting in that gaze. Beholding that we are being lovingly beheld—that's a human experience we all long for, and when it happens, we never forget it.

I know I'll never forget the first time it happened to me.

I had been away at school for a year. Actually, it was my first year at the Franciscan seminary. In those days, many of us went to the seminary right after grade school, and that was my first time away from home. Needless to say, it was also a year away from girls.

When they heard that I was coming back for the summer, my old gang decided to throw a party, with Dickie (as I was called then) as the guest of honor. So there we were, boys and girls, all feeling a little awkward. The boys were huddled on one side of the room, and the girls were standing on the other.

I remember one girl, especially. Her name was Bonnie. She had been in my eighth grade class, and I was thinking I would really like to dance with her, but I figured she would have forgotten all about me. Finally I got up the courage to look across the room to where she was standing—and there she was, looking straight at me!

I didn't know what to do! I quickly looked down at my feet, feeling all excited and flustered at the same time. I was breathing hard, my mouth was dry and my palms were sweating. Was she really looking at me, I wondered? I couldn't believe it was true. She must have just been looking around and happened to catch me looking at her.

But what if she *was* looking at me? My heart was in my throat. What should I do? Finally, hoping against hope, I looked up again—and she was still looking at me! I felt so alive and happy that I forgot about myself and went over and talked with her. That look of love melted my fear, and after a while I even asked her to dance.

The whole summer I just lived on that look of love. Things that otherwise would have been a pain were no bother at all. Because somebody looked at me with love in her eyes, all the rest was easy to take.

If you know somebody loves you, you know you're lovable. Your life has meaning. You have something to live for. And nothing that happens can take it away. It gives you a sustaining power that supports and liberates you.

In prayer we discover that God is looking at us with that very same look of love. Maybe at first we don't believe it. We can't see why he should be loving us, but every time we look up we find him still loving us, and finally we begin to realize it's true. That realization is a joy and a freedom and an energy. It puts a power in our lives not just for a summer but for a lifetime.

And yet a single look of love from God cannot sustain us forever. We forget. Our experience of communion with the Lord in prayer may energize us for a while, but prayer in the long run has to be an ongoing dialogue so that we can keep in touch with the source of our power. Our relationship with the Lord in prayer must be a constant one, just as Mary's was.

Practically speaking, though, how does one move into this prayer relationship? St. Francis of Assisi found that the best way to do it was through praise. Just find something to be thankful for, and move into it. So Francis went through life from day to day always finding new reasons to praise God. Whatever happened, good or bad, important or insignificant, he praised God for it. Whatever he saw, beautiful or ugly, unique or commonplace, he praised God for it. He praised God for the sun when it was shining, for the rain when it was not. He praised God for health when he had it, for illness when he did not. He praised God for the people who loved him and the people who despised him. He praised God for the animals and the birds, for the trees and the flowers, even for the grass and the stones on the ground. He did not try to earn God's love. He did not even try to find it. Instead he simply celebrated it, finding reasons to do so in everything around him. By doing that, he became ever more aware of the love that he was celebrating, and so moved into prayer.

The liturgy contains a great deal of praise, or at least the vestiges of it. The Glory to God in the Highest, the Holy, Holy, Holy and many other prayers were all originally, and are meant to be, shouts of praise. But praising and thanking God does not have to be done in a group. You can do it with just one other person, or by yourself, at home, at work, in school, riding on the bus, driving the car, walking—really, any place and any time.

Eventually, however, praise gives way to communion with the Goodness we are praising. It gives rise to a kind of prayer that I would describe as resting in the presence of the One who loves us and attentively listening to what God wants to teach us. This kind of prayer involves both delighting in God's love and trusting in God's word. We let ourselves become aware of God's loving presence, and then slowly we also become aware of God's loving wisdom being spoken in our hearts.

First of all, then, prayer means resting and waiting. Mary (the sister of Martha) is the woman waiting on the Lord. She is not busy, she is not concerned with being efficient. Prayer is as inefficient as being in love. It is being, not doing. It is resting, not acting. It is delighting in the presence of the lover. It is wanting just to be there, knowing that it is the right place to be. It is recognizing and loving the Presence that wants nothing from us but presence.

But, secondly, prayer moves into an *expectant* waiting. It becomes an attentive listening to the Lord, a readiness to say yes whenever God should speak. It moves into a mode of discernment, wanting to discover what the lover wants of us and eager to respond. Here prayer is a listening with the heart, a hearing with the hidden ear, a learning within the soul. And when the Lord's will is revealed for us, we accept it as our own. We affirm it because we desire nothing but to please the lover. We believe it because God's word is truth and life. We trust it because we know God loves us and wants only the best for us. When we trust God we are never disappointed.

From praying in faith, we can then move to acting in faith. After hearing God's will we must be obedient to what we have heard. We must step out in faith, stand on God's promise, claim the victory, walk like we talk and celebrate God's love. This is not the same as doing something that we want to do and adding, as an afterthought, "if it be your will." It is saying, as Mary did, "Let it be done according to your word." It is saying beforehand, as Jesus did in Gethsemane, "Your will be done," and then acting in accordance with what the Lord has told us to do.

Such prayer, and such acting in faith, can seem bold and falsely self-assured to people who have not experienced it. And in fact it can become proud and arrogant unless we remain in the dialogue of prayer. We can never say, "God wills it," and then go merrily on our way as though that was all there is to it. We can never go stepping all over people in order to accomplish what we heard God telling us to do yesterday. God is with us always in the present, and God speaks to us only in the now.

With every step, then, we must listen again, seeking always to discern God's will in the present moment.

The femininity of constant openness redeems us from the arrogance of masculine action. Mary's glory was her virginity, her grace was her emptiness. The saving grace of the woman and the man of prayer is the knowledge of their nothingness. The constant awareness that God is everything and we are nothing calls us ever into dialogue with the love that gives us the power to step out in faith. And the constant willingness to risk and to act keeps our prayer from becoming mere illusion or self-gratification.

The Church at Prayer

Prayer is often private, a personal dialogue between ourselves and God. Jesus commended private prayer by telling his disciples not to pray like show-offs in public, but instead to pray to the Father when no one else is watching (Matthew 6:5-6). Jesus also taught the value of private prayer by his own example, often staying up at night or going off into the hills by himself to pray.

But prayer is also communal, an experience of praying together as sons and daughters to a common Father. Communal prayer is important because it is usually our first introduction to any type of prayer at all. We often learn to pray by joining in a community of prayer, and only later do we discover that we can do alone what as children we did in a group.

The great shortcoming of common prayer is that it can often become the sort of hypocritical show which Jesus warned his disciples about. People can go through the external motions of prayer without entering into the internal dialogue which is the essence of prayer. More often than not this is an unintentional hypocrisy committed by people who have never really learned to pray privately and so they have nothing to bring to their efforts at communal worship. But the result is the same: stale, listless, repetitive words which never become true prayer.

True prayer is what the scriptures call "prayer in the

Spirit." St. Paul refers to the Spirit's presence in our prayer as the one who breathes life into it. When we surrender to God in prayer, it is as though the Holy Spirit takes over our human spirit in some way and makes up for our shortcomings:

> The Spirit also helps us in our weakness. For when
> we do not know what to say in prayer, the Spirit
> expresses what we mean in wordless sounds and
> sighs. And since the Father knows our hearts, he
> understands what the Spirit is saying in us, for the
> Spirit in us always prays the way God wants us to.
> (Romans 8:26-27)

In our trinitarian theology we say that the Spirit proceeds from the Father and the Son. That can seem like just so many words when we recite them in the Creed on Sunday, but the theological idea probably arose out of the experience of prayer which Paul is talking about. When we assemble as the body of Christ for worship, the Spirit is that dialogue, that going back and forth, that relationship of love given and received, between ourselves and the Father. It is a powerful energy which is neither Father nor the community, but something flowing between them which enables them to relate to one another. The trinitarian life is now repeated in and through us.

This can be an intoxicating experience. Paul admonishes one of his community to forget about getting drunk on wine and experience instead a new kind of drunkenness:

> Be filled with the Holy Spirit. When you are together,
> speak in the words of psalms and hymns with
> inspired melodies. Then sing praise to the Lord with
> all your hearts, so that you go on always and
> everywhere to give thanks to God who is our Father
> in the name of our Lord Jesus Christ.
> (Ephesians 5:18-20)

I never would have really understood what Paul was talking about if I had not seen it happen in our own community. One time there were 75 young women from New Jerusalem making a retreat together in our mansion. Every time someone opened the door of a room they were in, singing came floating out. Hour after hour they were finding new reasons for praising God and celebrating God's goodness. Sometimes their meal got cold while they kept on singing in the Spirit, but we knew it didn't matter. We Marthas remembered the Lord's words to Mary that only one thing is really necessary. Those Marys at prayer had found the best part, and we were not about to take it away from them.

Even Paul recognized, however, that sometimes praying in the Spirit can get out of hand. When it does, some other spirit is taking over. It may be a spirit of individualism, with some people imposing their own wants and needs on the group. It may be a spirit of jealousy, of anger, of impatience, or whatever, in others. It may just be a general spirit of aimlessness. It may even be a spirit of excited overenthusiasm, so that praying is going on but the prayer seems to be moving nowhere.

From time to time in his letters, therefore, Paul suggests some order for praying in community, for "God is not a God of confusion but of peace" (1 Corinthians 12:33). The idea is not that all prayer meetings have to follow the format Paul describes, but that when Christians are praying as a body there should be some order among the members. The energy of praying in the Spirit needs to coalesce in the same way into a unified, communal prayer experience.

Paul's concern seems to be just the opposite of most liturgists and celebrants who want to awaken the sleepyheads in the pews, not control their enthusiasm. Our liturgies are so well structured that we hardly ever feel the Spirit bursting forth!

But the problem is not primarily with the Mass. The deeper problem is that when people are not individually persons of prayer, they have little or nothing with which to fill the formal structure of the liturgy. Unless Christians are continually in dialogue with God, they cannot join their personal dialogue with that of others into an experience of communal dialogue. If that relationship of surrender and support is not continuously going on in people's private lives, they cannot experience that relationship together in their public worship.

When we assemble to pray as Church, therefore, we need

126

to be an assembly of praying Christians. We need to come together as a body of people who are already praying in the Spirit and living in the Spirit, doing as the Father is directing us in our daily lives. There is no substitute for that. Trying to make liturgy "work" without that is trying to make bread without dough. Our Eucharist cannot become the body of Christ offered to the Father unless the grains of wheat assembled there know what it means to die with Jesus and rise in the Spirit.

All too often people in families, priests in rectories, sisters in convents and even monks in monasteries have not really laid their lives down for one another in the way that Jesus has taught us. They have not experienced in their own small communities what communal worship is supposed to celebrate. Or if they have, they have not reflected on their personal experience of sacrificing themselves for one another so that they can connect it with the sacrifice of the Mass.

All too often Catholics have not really laid their souls bare before one another in experiences of small-group prayer. When we don't expose our faith to even a small circle of friends who know us, it is very difficult to express our faith in a larger gathering. When we don't thank God out loud for our everyday blessings, it is hard to sing out God's praise when we come together on Sunday.

In the end, therefore, we come back to the beginning. We come back to the image of Mary, the empty virgin waiting to be filled by the power of the Holy Spirit. The "woman" is the prototype of every Christian, feminine before the Lord, wanting only to do his will. She is as well the archetype of every Christian community, expecting the Spirit to come over it in prayer.

The "virgin" is the empty one, whose openness to God is both her grace and her glory. She is the Mary, not the Martha, who opens up the space to listen to the Lord. We all need spaces of silence in our lives, so that we can hear what God is telling us. Words on a page make no sense unless there are spaces between them. Lives full of busyness become a blur unless they are brought into focus during prayer. In prayer we find the meaning of our lives, both the meaning that they have and the meaning that they ought to have. Prayer creates that virginal space in which the Lord can speak to us and show us the direction of our lives.

The only way to pray well is to pray much. St. Paul tells us that we should pray constantly (Ephesians 6:18), that we should be in constant dialogue with God. Mary, the virgin and mother, is the personification of that dialogue. As virgin she is the exemplar of its receptiveness. As mother, she is the model of its fruitfulness. Only the feminine receives the seed which becomes the incarnate Christ.

CHAPTER FIVE

Paul:
A New Creation

$\mathbf{P}$aul, the great apostle to the gentiles, is a unique figure in the New Testament. Almost half of the books in the New Testament bear his name, either because he actually wrote them or because other early Christians knew that the name of Paul was so well respected in the Church that they attached his name to their work rather than their own. Even the Epistle to the Hebrews, which does not bear the name of any author, was for many centuries believed to have been written by Paul.

Scripture scholars using modern linguistic methods of analysis identify these letters as genuinely Pauline because they were all written by the same person: Thessalonians, Corinthians, Romans, Galatians, Philippians and Philemon. Either one or both of the letters to the Colossians and the Ephesians may have been written by a disciple of Paul who knew Paul's theology and style of writing. But the letters to Timothy and Titus were probably written long after Paul's martyrdom in Rome around 65 A.D., perhaps by a member of one of the communities that Paul had founded.

Paul himself was a well-educated Jew born and raised outside of Palestine. He used his Hebrew name Saul when he was among his fellow Jews and his Greek name Paul when he worked among gentiles. As a member of the Pharisee movement, he was a very religious man even before his conversion to Christianity. The Pharisees were strict observers of the Torah, and they believed that salvation came through piously fulfilling every detail of the Mosaic Law. Paul was such a zealous Pharisee that he participated in the persecution of those Jews who claimed that Jesus was the messiah. In the Book of Acts, we read about one such persecution which ended in the martyrdom of Stephen. While Stephen was being stoned to death for blasphemy, Paul stood by and watched approvingly:

> "The witnesses laid their robes at the feet of a young man named Saul." (Acts 7:58)

Not long afterwards Paul was on his way to Damascus to ferret out believers in Jesus in the Jewish community there. No doubt he believed he was doing the right thing, but something quite unexpected changed his plans:

> It happened that while he was traveling to Damascus and approaching the city, suddenly a light from heaven shone all around him. He fell to the ground, and then he heard a voice saying, "Saul, Saul, why are you persecuting me?" "Who are you, Lord?" he asked, and the answer came, "I am Jesus, whom you are persecuting." (Acts 9:3-5 NJB)

In that single experience Paul learned two things that changed his life forever. First, Paul learned that God comes to us and meets us where we are to offer us salvation. God's love is a totally free and unexpected gift. Salvation is never earned but is always grace. Second, Paul learned that there is such a deep unity between Christians and their savior that to persecute the one is to persecute the other. Paul thought that Jesus was dead and that there was no connection between him and his scattered followers. But he learned that Jesus is alive and living in the body of believers where his Spirit dwells.

It would be impossible to even summarize all that is in Paul's epistles, those long letters which he wrote to Christians in the early Church. What we can do, though, is pull together much of what he says around two basic themes—the themes which he first heard sounded in his own conversion experience. By reflecting on that experience during his years of apostolic work, he developed many of his theological ideas. Very often they revolved around the theme of grace, salvation and justification by faith and the theme of the Church as that body of Christ which is made one by the Holy Spirit.

Salvation and Justification

Catholics often think of salvation as something that will happen after they die, if they've been good and obeyed the commandments. It is true that there is some reference to future salvation in the New Testament, but the main emphasis in the gospels and the epistles is that salvation begins *now*, and after that it can go on forever.

For Paul, salvation is something that is experienced. He wrote about the experience in so many ways, trying to get a handle on it, trying to put into words something for which he had no ready-made vocabulary. He used phrases such as *new creation* in trying to describe it. He wrote to the Galatians at one point, "All that matters is to be created anew" (Galatians 6:15). He himself felt like a new man after his conversion, filled with a new power he had never known before. It was the power to fulfill the spirit of the Jewish Law without having to worry about every letter of the Law. It was the power of the Spirit who had inspired the Law, but who is greater than the Law itself.

Many Christians today have never experienced the power of that Spirit within them, which is why they try to earn salvation by carefully observing the laws of God and the Church—much as the Pharisees did. That way of living is not bad, but it is incomplete. It is not the way of the prophets, it is not the way of Jesus, and it is not the way of the Spirit. Nor is it the way that Paul experienced and wrote about.

When we first hear the word *salvation* in the context of religion, we may even wonder what it means. I can remember thinking when I was a boy that I didn't need to be saved. After all, I wasn't drowning, or in a burning building! I felt pretty safe already. And adults today, sitting comfortably in church, might rightly wonder why all this fuss about salvation. They feel pretty contented, pretty safe. If they think of salvation in religious terms, they may even feel secure in their observance of the moral law. Never having seen the magnificence of the ocean, they're satisfied with their pretty little swimming pool.

For Paul observance of the Law was the beginning of his realization of the meaning of salvation. Salvation had come to Israel through the covenant, and through the observance of God's commandments. The same happens to us in our own lives. We begin by being told by our parents what to do and what not to do. We don't fully understand why it's right to do some things and why it's wrong to do others. We only know that our parents love us, and so we trust them and do as we are told.

But law is not an end in itself. It's a means to an end. The rules our parents give us are a means of living safely. That is why they tell us, "Don't play with matches," and, "Look both ways before crossing the street." The laws in our society give us the means to live safely and fairly with others. What would our lives be like if no one obeyed traffic signals or if everyone felt free to cheat and steal? Law is a means to salvation of a sort, on a very basic human level.

What law does, however, is just make us aware of the problem. It gives a certain basic order to society, a framework within which people can live their lives. But what if people just obeyed the law and nothing more? Is there any law that you have to make friends? Is there any law that you have to fall in love? Is there any law that you have to succeed, or accomplish anything, or be happy? Is there any law that when you are suffering, people have to care about you? Of course there isn't. Almost everything that makes life enjoyable and satisfying comes from people going beyond the legal minimum. It's going beyond the letter of the law that makes life worth living: "The letter kills but the Spirit gives life" (2 Corinthians 3:7).

The same is true in our spiritual life. The framework of the commandments provides a basic regularity in our spiritual life that we need if we are ever to grow beyond the commandments and discover the beatitudes. We can't expect to be blessed with the happiness of living in the reign of God if we never obey God's laws. Yet even God's laws are not an end in themselves. Living within them simply frees us to hear the call of the Spirit to the more radical spiritual life of the beatitudes.

Law is something good, it can come from God and, at a certain level, we can even say it gives life. The Israelites experienced the Decalogue as a God-given good. The Torah was an ordered way of life that was so much better than the bitterness of slavery, so much better than not knowing God and having no meaning in life. The laws that they received from Moses taught them, like children, how to honor God and respect one another, even if they did not understand the ultimate purpose behind all those rules.

But such "code morality" in itself fails to become an internalized force for doing good. It often fails to discern real good and evil. It remains an external set of norms—"Do this." "Don't do that."—which often keeps people in spiritual infancy and moral childhood. Eventually code morality even defeats the very purpose for which it was given. Instead of giving people the social stability they need to go beyond the law in doing good for one another, the law becomes the most that people are willing to do without being coerced. Instead of giving people the inner stability they need to listen to God calling them to an ever richer life, the law becomes a rigid standard of ethics to be scrupulously adhered to. They no longer listen, learn, grow or even pray for wisdom. They just obey laws and feel justified in that.

In the end, then, code morality becomes an illusion. It becomes a substitute for spiritual growth and moral adulthood. It takes the place of surrendering your life to God, trusting God to lead you beyond your comfortable security, and living in the Spirit. This is why religion and Church sometimes stifle the Spirit and keep people locked in moral immaturity. If they do not invite people to a personal dialogue with the living God, they become an end in themselves.

Paul was quite aware of all this, which is why he insisted over and over again that the Jewish Law is not Christian morality. The Law is the beginning of morality, but it is not what living in the Lord is ultimately all about. He was a good man, and a very good Jew, but in meeting Jesus personally he discovered that there was so much more to life than just being good. It was like moving out of childhood and into adulthood, moving out of blind obedience and into personal dialogue:

When I was a child, I used to talk like a child, think like a child, and reason like a child. But when I became an adult, I put those childish ways behind me. Now we see as though we were looking through a darkened glass; later we shall see more clearly. Now I partly understand; later I shall understand more fully, the way God fully understands. But in the meantime, what we have are faith, hope and love. And the most important of these is love.

(1 Corinthians 13:11-13)

For those who are following the Spirit's lead, things are often not as clear as they are for those who are just following the law. We live the life of faith, trusting in the Lord and not our own perfection. We hope in his promise, believing that we will not be disappointed (see Philippians 3:6-15). And above all, we live in loving relationship with God and with others, knowing only that no matter how good or how sinful we are we all live under the total mercy and forgiveness of God.

The life of faith is risky business. The life of hope is an adventurous dream. The life of love is always full of crucifixions. As St. Paul put it, we work toward our salvation "in fear and trembling" (Philippians 2:12). For we no longer have the security of always having the law on our side. We no longer have the comfort of always knowing we are right. We cannot retain the false sense of being moral or in control by adhering to a few precepts.

This is the crucial difference between the usual understanding of Old Testament morality and St. Paul's understanding of New Testament morality, between living within the confines of the commandments and living in the freedom of the Spirit. It is the difference between law and love, between religion and faith, between merit and grace. It is the passage from childhood to adulthood, from self-control to self-surrender, from code morality to personal relationship with others and with the Lord. It doesn't always have the luxury of looking right or feeling "holy."

The way of faith is difficult to find because the path is narrow and the gate is small, as Jesus put it. So many walk along the broad road of religion and completely miss the salvation that Paul is speaking of. It's easy to be satisfied with going to church and not breaking the commandments. It's easy to be satisfied with going through the motions that we think will "get us into heaven." The opposite of real faith is most often not atheism but religiosity.

It is only in the relationship of faith that we experience true salvation or, as Paul often calls it in the Epistle to the Romans, justification. It's a kind of straightening out of our lives that comes by not trying to do just that! For trying to do that on our own only confuses the issue and keeps us measuring our perfection instead of surrendering to God's love. Until we make that surrender, what we think of as salvation is actually preventing us from being saved. What we believe is justification is actually self-justification. What seems like fulfillment is actually the absence of fulfillment; but not knowing the real thing, we mistake it for the real thing.

When we're involved with mere religion, we're often satisifed because we think we are fulfilling the law. But actually, the law of Christ can never be fulfilled. Jesus gave his followers only one commandment, to love as he loved, to love in total self-surrender and vulnerability, even as he did. We can never stand before the Lord and say we have completely fulfilled that one commandment. He is always calling us to love more deeply and more fully and more perfectly.

Even if we try to fulfill that law by our own efforts, we don't succeed. And if we try to fulfill it by doing good things for God, we still don't succeed. But God does not ask us for success; God asks only for our surrender.

Sometimes it is only in the experience of failure that we learn to surrender to God. When we fail to fulfill the law of Christ, we can discover that we need God to love through us. When we fail to fulfill the commandments on our own, we can find out how much we need God's personal presence in our lives. In that sense, Paul saw the commandments and the Law as a preparation for salvation. In our experience of failing and falling and fumbling, we are led to trust. In our experience of defeat, we allow the Lord to pick us up and give us his victory. That is why Paul loves to say that it is "When we are weak that

135

we are strong" (2 Corinthians 12:10).

For Paul, then, and for every person of faith, salvation is totally from God and justification is totally gift. It is all grace. Grace is everything. We cannot merit it; we cannot earn it (Ephesians 2:6-9). We can only ask for it, receive it and celebrate it. It is God who always saves us, justifies us and redeems us. They are all the same thing, just different words trying to express the experience of allowing God to love us, letting ourselves be filled with that love and sharing it with others.

Through his unique conversion, and even before he learned about Jesus from the Christian community, Paul experienced the meaning of Jesus' teaching that we discover new life only through surrendering the old. Letting go of our self is the only way to the renewal of the self. Radical obedience to the Spirit is the only means to spiritual freedom.

Living under such obedience sets us free from conformity to others. If we are each listening to the Lord, following where the Spirit leads us, our journeys are bound to be different from each other. Yet we can walk our separate ways in unity, if we are united in the Spirit. Jesus prayed for unity among his followers, not uniformity. When we are deeply commited to following the Lord, the Spirit gives us different gifts which work together in the unity of service to one another (Ephesians 4:11-13).

If we seek salvation through obedience to the law, obedience to Christ becomes secondary. On the contrary, if we are obedient to Christ and allow him to save us, the law becomes secondary. We are free to follow it gladly, since some law also comes from God. But we are set free from following it slavishly, even as Jesus was free not to follow the Jewish Law slavishly—to the consternation of the Pharisees. Those who do not live in a personal relationship with God do not understand this paradox. They do not see how obedience can be liberating. But those who live in radical obedience to Christ receive the only freedom that ultimately matters. They receive the freedom to submit to the law whenever its demands are just, and the freedom to move beyond the confines of the law when its demands constrict the real demands of Christ's gospel.

Thus Paul says, after he has set out on the journey of faith and has experienced the liberation of Jesus:

> As far as the Law can make a person just, I was perfect. But because of Christ, I have come to consider this advantage as a disadvantage. Not only that, but it all seems worthless when compared to the supreme advantage of knowing Christ Jesus my Lord. For his sake I have accepted the loss of everything I once valued, and I even count it as garbage so that I might have a relationship of unity with Christ. I am no longer striving to be justified by my own efforts, which is the justification that comes from the Law. Now I want only the justification that comes through faith in Christ, which is from God and is based on trust. (Philippians 3:6-9)

For Paul, then, salvation comes through a personal relationship with Christ, and justification comes through a trusting faith in God and not in ourselves. If we left it at that, however, redemption could seem to be very individualistic—a Jesus-and-me type of religion with no connection to the Church. It could seem to be that brand of fundamentalism which is proclaimed by television preachers to millions of viewers who have no relationship to one another. But this is not Paul's understanding of redemption. For him, salvation and justification occur primarily through our connectedness with Christ in a body of believers.

The Body of Christ

Paul the Apostle was the first great missionary of Christianity. He was the first to carry the good news of salvation by Christ and justification by faith throughout most of the Roman Empire. We are sure, then, that he preached. And we are sure that he baptized. But he did not believe that preaching and baptizing was all there is to evangelization. He did not claim that believing in God and accepting Jesus as Lord is all it takes to be saved, as some modern evangelists do. Instead, he used a strategy which was very incarnational. Wherever he preached and baptized he also formed and nourished a body of believers to support and serve one another.

Paul referred to any community that he founded as a "body of Christ." It was not just a collection of individuals who all believed in Jesus, but it was a unified social body whose members worked together and helped one another in many ways. It was a body whose head was not Paul but Christ, for Christ remained the head even after Paul left to establish another community. It was a body whose spirit was not Paul's but Christ's, for each of the members received the Holy Spirit through baptism and the laying on of hands. Because it was a community with a single head and a single spirit, Paul could call it a body. And because its head and spirit were Christ's, Paul could call it a body of Christ.

When Protestants hear the phrase *body of Christ*, they often think of it metaphorically: the Church is *like* a body of Christ. When Catholics hear that phrase, they often think of it metaphysically: the whole Church really *is* the body of Christ, but it is an unexperienced "mystical" reality. But Paul's usage of the phrase is neither metaphorical, metaphysical nor mystical; it is *incarnational*. He is thinking about flesh and blood people who are drawn together by their personal surrender to Christ as Lord and whose lives are vibrant with the power of the Holy Spirit.

Paul sums up his mission and his vision of the Church in his letter to the Colossians:

> I am glad to suffer for you, and in doing so I am enduring what has yet to be suffered by Christ for the sake of his body, the Church. I became a servant of the Church when I accepted the divine task of helping you to fulfill the word of God. That word is a mystery which was hidden for generations but which was recently revealed to those whom God made holy. Furthermore, God wanted them to spread the word about the glorious riches of this hidden reality to the gentiles as well. The mystery is Christ

in you, who is your hope of glory. This is the Christ that we proclaim. We tell everyone all there is to know about this mystery, and we instruct them so that they can become mature in Christ. (Colossians 1:24-28)

The Christ that Paul proclaims here is not a man who died in Judea perhaps 30 years before but the Lord who lives by the power of God in every body of believers that incarnates his Spirit. The glory of the risen Christ is the glory that Christians have a foretaste of as they live in the Spirit, as they await the Second Coming and final resurrection. The mystery is something that was unknown to previous generations but which is now known to all those who experience it in their life together. It is a secret that can be taught, but learning it means more than just hearing about it: It entails instruction and development into a living organism.

When Paul speaks of the risen Christ, therefore, he does not have in mind a person who has gone to heaven. And when he speaks of Christ in the Church, he does not mean something like an invisible man walking around in the community. Christ is present precisely in the community itself. He is present in the sharing of gifts and the laying down of lives for one another. With Christ as the head of a new body, miraculous things happen, just as they did for Jesus. With the Lord as the center of a new unity, God's love is poured out, just as it was from Jesus. With the Spirit as the power in the Church, divine energy explodes into the world, just as it did through Jesus.

Though many people call themselves Christians, the majority of them have never experienced this mystery. They have never known the unity with each other which knits them into a body of Christ. They have never together surrendered to his Lordship nor been filled together by his Spirit. But this is precisely the mystery of salvation, the secret of being drawn together into a unity which heals and strengthens and gives life to each of its members. It is the secret which the first disciples discovered through living with Jesus and learning from him. It is the secret which the first Jewish community experienced through their reception of the Spirit at Pentecost and their living through the power of that Spirit afterwards. It is the secret which can now be known to anyone who becomes immersed in the living body of Christ.

Christianity is essentially community. In the history of the Church this truth has been discovered and rediscovered by religious communities. The hermits who went out into the desert to find the Lord eventually gathered together to live close to one another. In these first monastic communities they found a presence of Christ and a power of the Spirit that they could not find alone. Each monastic renewal through the centuries has been a recovery of the original unity which had somehow gotten lost. Those who gathered around St. Francis, St. Clare and the founders of the many other religious orders found a life and vitality in community which was so attractive that it naturally drew others into it. It was a clear alternative to the systems of the world: a new social order not based on power, prestige and possessions, but on disinterested, divine love.

I believe it was Cardinal Suenens who once said that to be a Christian is to live in such a way that our life does not make sense if God does not exist. That's a drastic way to put it, but it emphasizes the radical calling that Christianity really is. Our life together should be so grounded in Christ's presence and energized by his Spirit that people cannot understand it in human terms. When they see us they should ask: Why are they so different from us? Where do they get that power from? What draws them together? What leads them on? Why can they live in a way that we cannot?

When people see that power and that life of Christ, they are naturally drawn to it. They see the evidence of the Spirit in our lives, and they want to be immersed in it. They don't have to be preached to; they want to be baptized. They want to enter into the alternative that they see so evidently before them. All they need is to be told that the death and resurrection of Jesus has made it possible for us to live in this new way, based on an initial death which Paul called baptism (Romans 6).

Too often, however, we belong to parishes and religious orders and other Catholic institutions which are not bodies of Christ in this living, existential sense. Instead we surround ourselves with props of religiosity and symbols of security. We have all sorts of things that tell us we are right and that make us comfortable, and then we are no different from anybody else. Just the opposite of St. Peter in the Book of Acts, we tell the world, "Gold and silver we have plenty of, but we cannot say stand up and walk in the name of Jesus."

When are we a body of Christ in the Pauline sense? There are many ways we could define it, but perhaps it's better if instead we identify three telling signs.

Jesus as Our Lord

First, we are a body of Christ when Jesus is our Lord, not individually but together. When Jesus is our head and we are his members, we recognize that the new life that we've found together comes from him and flows from him. St. Paul describes this eloquently in the First Letter to the Corinthians, chapter 12. You can easily see what he is talking about if you imagine a hand that has been severed from a body. For a while it will still look like a hand, but unconnected to the head, it cannot move, it cannot live, it cannot be the member that it's supposed to be.

Likewise when people try to be Christians without having a personal relationship to Jesus, they may look like Christians but they really do not have the life which flows from being connected to him and obeying his direction. Either Jesus is our Lord, or he is not. If he is not, we are letting other things direct and motivate us. If he is, then we let him call the shots. We let him lead us to sacrifice ourselves for the sake of the Church and for the sake of the world. We let him lead us in faith, trusting that each death he asks of us will lead to resurrection.

Jesus as Our Life

Second, we are a body of Christ when Jesus is our life, again not singly but in community. It does not have to be life in a religious order. It does not have to be a life of total dedication to some worthy cause or work of charity. It can and should be a life that is found in families, in Church and school groups, on the job or just with friends. It only has to be a life of love. It has to be the love of Christ, loving through us. It has to be what the New Testament calls *agape*: self-giving, unrestricted and inclusive love. Jesus' life is all-embracing, without divisions, without enemies.

141

Ordinary human love tends to be self-seeking: We love someone or something for what they can give to us. It tends to be restricted: We love only as long as we get what we want. And it tends to be exclusive: We love possessively, jealously guarding what we have and keeping others away from it. But *agape* love is that gift from God which is the very love that Jesus loved others with, and that God loves us with. It is the love of God that is the very life of God and the life of the Christian community.

Agape is also the love that we love God with. The love with which we love one another in community and the love with which we love God in our personal relationship with the Lord is exactly the same love. All these loves are one and the same, the gift of love which comes from God, which flows through us and returns to God in prayer. St. John had this very incarnational sense of God's love when he wrote:

> My dear friends,
> let us love each other,
> since love is from God
> and everyone who loves is a child of God and knows
>   God.
> Whoever fails to love does not know God,
> because God is love....
> Anyone who says, "I love God"
> and hates his brother,
> is a liar,
> since whoever does not love the brother whom he
>   can see
> cannot love God whom he has not seen.
>   (1 John 4:7-8, 20 NJB)

The love which is spoken of here is *agape*, the love which is the life of God, the love which flows between the Father and the Son and pours out as the Holy Spirit. When that love flows between brothers and sisters in community, it is the life of God. It shows itself in a lack of concern for security, rightness, power, money, image, control—those things we often identify our "self" with. It is the life with which Jesus lived, which he poured out

142

in love, and which was and still is received as the Spirit of new life.

One time about 40 of us in New Jerusalem spent a day getting ready for Christmas together: preparing food and baking cookies, putting up decorations, trimming trees. We worked until about 11 o'clock that night, and then we gathered to celebrate the Eucharist. That Mass must have lasted about an hour and a half. It was so obvious to all of us that there was a sharing of common life among us. In terms of our spiritual growth and our understanding of the Lord, we were probably in many different places. But there was a spirit and an energy, a love and a life, passing between us. There was a unity we could all experience. To us it was so clearly the sharing of a single life, the life of a single person, Christ our Lord.

Living that shared life naturally calls for celebration, and spills over into it. The celebration of that life is what the Eucharist is all about. But we do not have to wait for religious rituals to celebrate that life. It should burst out in smiles and hugs whenever we are with each other. It is because I have seen it with my own eyes and felt it with my own heart that I know what *agape* is all about. It is different than just being nice. It has an entirely different energy.

Jesus as Our Lover
Third, we are a body of Christ when Jesus is our lover. The New Testament calls Jesus the bridegroom of the Church. What a wonderfully sensuous image that is! But it has to be true both of all of us together and of each of us singly. Together we love the Lord, and that's what makes us one. Together we are his bride and he is our lover, inviting us to love him in himself and in one another at the same time. To love Christ is to love the Church; they are not two separate loves.

But to love the Church with the love of Christ, we must also each have a personal love relationship with Jesus. Both celibates and married people can often forget this. We have an affective need that is so great that it cannot be met by saying, "I love my work," or, "I love my family."

Celibates especially are prone to deny that need for affection, to get lost in their work, and to forget their prayer life.

But every person needs a lover. Every man and woman needs to love deeply and emotionally, and to receive that love in return. If we who are single do not have Jesus as our lover, where will that affective need be met? Without a personal relationship of love with Jesus, experienced in the dialogue of prayer, celibacy is at best foolish and at worst dangerous.

Even those of us who are married know that our deep affective need cannot always be met by our spouses. Married people need the same relationship of love to Christ that celibates do.

In community, however, we experience the love of Christ not only in our prayer life but also in our community life. Our affective need to give and receive love is met not only in our personal relationship with the Lord but also in our personal relationships with one another. We are living a full Christian life only when we feel the love of Jesus coming to us both when we are united with him in prayer and when we are in unity with our sisters and brothers in the Lord. He loves us through the people that we live with, not just in a one-to-one relationship.

All too often teenagers try to satisfy their awakening need for affective love by going steady. They cling to one relationship for months and even years, and you can just see them starving on the vine. At the time in their life when they should be experiencing the most growth, their personality is not growing at all because it is locked into an exclusive, jealously guarded relationship.

That is a major reason why we see the breakdown of so many marriages in our society today. Too many young people have not been trained how to love. As St. Paul said, they need to be instructed "so that they can become mature in Christ" (Colossians 4:28). They have not learned the discipline of love by being disciples of the Lord in a loving Christian community. It is virtually impossible to know what it means to lay down your life for one person over and over again until you've learned to do it many times for many people. *Agape* love is a special gift that comes from the Lord, but in my experience it comes mainly through the body of Christ. We may receive a special surge of *agape* when we are baptized in the Spirit, but too many "born again" Christians become "dead again" Christians unless their

144

ability to love is nurtured and developed through community living.

We are the body of Christ, therefore, when Jesus is our Lord, our life and our lover. The body of Christ is a concrete, here-and-now, experienced unity, composed of real people who are living and working together, trusting the Lord and laying their lives down for one another. It implies membership in a larger community such as the Catholic Church, and even in the cosmic unity of all Christians past and present which is called the Communion of Saints. But a larger unity cannot be composed of nonexistent parts. A real universal unity has to be built on real local unity.

Paul wrote to the Church in Thessalonica, the Church in Galatia, the Church in Corinth and other local Churches. Almost all of the New Testament authors had some particular community in mind when they wrote their gospels and letters. Ultimately each of these communities was united, through their unity in Christ, with the universal, "catholic" Church. But first they had to be the Church that they were, where they were, with the people in their own community.

In the same way we have to be a body of Christ in our own particular prayer groups, parishes, religious communities *before* we can claim authentic membership in the larger body. Most of our daily lives are not governed by what is said in papal encyclicals and episcopal pastorals. Sometimes Catholics seem to think that if they live in conformity with what the pope or bishop says on this or that issue, they are living fully Christian lives. But in real life, most of our Christianity is lived on the local level, in the nitty-gritty of personal relationships. And that's precisely where we have to meet and love the Lord, if we are to claim to be his body. That's precisely where we learn to pray, to lay down our lives and to forgive 70 times seven times. So that's precisely where salvation takes place, whenever it really takes place. Salvation, redemption, justification, living in the kingdom—it all happens in the body of Christ.

Becoming a New Creation

Through the Church, in the body of Christ, the Lord calls us to a new way of living, a new way of relating to God, to others and to the world. It is often hard for people to understand this because they have never experienced it. They do not see how they are any different as Christians or Catholics, except perhaps that they have a different set of religious beliefs. They do not feel any different from the people around them. They do not have a noticeably different life-style from the people that live in their neighborhood, go to school or work with them, walk past them on the street or in the mall.

And it's true: Most churchgoers are not much different from people who do not go to church. Churchgoers live in the world and go to church on Sunday much the same as other people go to concerts or plays for their weekly inspiration. But that is the opposite of the New Testament understanding of Church. The scriptural ideal is not to live in the world and go to church, but to live in the Church and go out to the world.

In sociological terms, the Church is meant to be a *counterculture*. It is a community whose way of living runs counter to the prevailing culture. It is a way of cooperating rather than competing, a way of giving rather than getting, a way of sharing rather than hoarding, a way of sacrifice rather than comfort, a way of faith rather than knowledge, a way of relationship rather than anonymity, a way of love rather than animosity. Through membership in the body of Christ, this way of living is a sharing in the life of Christ. This "Jesus way of living" is empowered by the Holy Spirit and communicated through a body which has Jesus as its Lord and head.

In scriptural terms, Christians are called to be *in the world but not of the world* (John 15:18-19; 17:14-18). Another way that the scriptures speak of it is being *saved from the world* (John 16:33). That is, those who live in the kingdom are saved from the anger and fear, the bitterness and jealousy, the possessiveness and power-seeking, as well as the many other destructive habits that people in the world are dominated by. Through living in a body of Christ, the followers of Jesus are freed from slavishly behaving the way so much of the world usually behaves.

In our own Catholic tradition, the religious orders were all founded on this vision of the body of Christ. The call to community is a vocation to a total way of life, to a way of relating to others as sisters and brothers in the Lord. It demands a person's full commitment to this group of people and to their mission of living in the kingdom and bringing it to the world. During the historical period when most of the great religious orders were founded, it seemed that embracing this vision meant renouncing family ties and living as celibates. Today, however, our renewed understanding of the biblical concept of virginity enables us to see that it applies to everyone who believes and prays, not just to celibates. And this broader appreciation of vocation allows us to see that all Christians are called to community, not just a special few who choose to remain unmarried.

Lest this seem like a farfetched vision, it is important to realize that there are communities like this, bodies of Christ in the biblical sense, in the Church today. Some are in the Catholic Church; some are in other denominations. Some are in the charismatic movement; some are activist communities. Some are composed of members of religious orders who have rediscovered the original vision of their founders. Some people in these new communities are unmarried; most are not. In the Third World there are tens of thousands of base Christian communities developing and joining themselves together.

What unites them all, what makes them all bodies of Christ, is that they share the same Spirit and acknowledge the same Lord. They have discovered that new way of relating to God and to one another which Paul called a new creation. They have become a new reality, radiating a new vitality into the world. They have something to share which is really good news. They have a life which is adventurous and out of the ordinary. They have a grace and a glory such as that which attracted disciples to Jesus. When you see such a body of Christ, you feel you have to say, along with Paul, that you have seen the Lord.

Making the Lord visible in the world is the essence of sacramentality. In contemporary theology we speak about Christ

147

as the sacrament of God, making the reality of the Father visible for all to see. We speak about the Church as the sacrament of Christ, making the reality of the Son visible in the world. And we speak about the seven traditional sacraments as sacraments of the Church, making the reality of the Spirit available for all to receive. Yet this new way of speaking just puts in modern terms the incarnational theology that was always the wisdom of the sacraments in the Church.

Take the Sacrament of Reconciliation, for example—or Penance, as we used to call it. In Catholic spirituality it has never been enough to ask God to forgive you in private so you can then go on your own individual way as though nothing had happened. You have to share your sinfulness with another human being, pray for discernment, be open to counseling, and receive God's forgiveness in a very down-to-earth, concrete and personal way. This is completely consistent with Paul's understanding of the body of Christ.

Too often, though, the incarnational aspect of the sacraments has been obscured by the institutional aspects. Instead of being a dialogue, Confession became a ritual. Instead of being freeing, Confession became a burden. Too often the humanizing aspect of the sacraments has been displaced by the canonical and legal aspects. Instead of being an encounter between persons, Confession became an anonymous telling of sins. Instead of being a reconciliation with a community, it became absolution by a priest speaking on behalf of God alone.

When we recover the incarnational meaning of the body of Christ, however, the sacraments come alive with human meaning. In a vital Christian community, people don't have to be told to go to Confession; they seek reconciliation with one another, through the pastor of the community if need be, whenever they realize that unity has been broken. Parents don't bring their children to Baptism to have a stain washed off their soul, but to begin their immersion in the new life of Christ that flows through the community. People don't come to Mass to fulfill an obligation or to watch the priest doing something for them; they come to share their fullness in the Lord with other members of the body and to celebrate the meaning of their life together.

Even a sacrament such as Holy Orders becomes more significant and attractive in a living body of Christ. It's amazing how many young people in New Jerusalem, for example, have considered the call to the priesthood and the religious life. And many have broadened the concept of vocation to consider the possibility of becoming missionaries or lay ministers. I never preached about vocations to the New Jerusalem community, but I remember one year especially when the crop we sent to the seminary astounded the Franciscans. Once young people experience the love of the body of Christ, they spontaneously want to share that good news with others.

It's so beautiful to hear young men and women in our community saying that they are perfectly willing to remain celibate for the sake of the kingdom. They stand at the beginning of their adulthood, free to choose marriage or celibacy, listening to the Lord to call them toward one path or the other. There's great joy in that freedom, and they share that joy with the rest of us.

The living reality of the body of Christ, with all its members joined to and serving one another, has also led us to a greater awareness of the variety of ministries in the Church. In the past, we Catholics loaded all of the ministries on the priest—except for the teaching of children, which we gave to the nuns. Yet that's so very far from the picture of ministry that Paul gives us when he speaks of the body of Christ. The vision he holds out is not that of one man with all the gifts doing everything for everybody else, but that of one Spirit working through different people and a variety of gifts doing all that needs to be done in the community:

> There are many different gifts, but it is always the same Spirit; there are many different ways of serving, but it is always the same Lord. There are many different forms of activity, but in everybody it is the same God who is at work in them all. The particular manifestation of the Spirit granted to each one is to be used for the general good. (1 Corinthians 12:4-7 NJB)

What is that general good? The traditional name for it is

salvation, but we often forget that the word *salvation* comes from the Latin *salus*, meaning health or healing. The early Christians said, "*Extra ecclesiam nulla salus,*" which is often translated as, "Outside the Church there is no salvation." But they were not saying you can't get to heaven unless you're a Catholic; they were describing their experience that the only place where lives could be really healed was in their community.

So the purpose of ministering to one another, using the gifts that God has given us, is salvation—the healing of lives. And as individual lives are healed, the body itself becomes more healthy. Thus Paul also spoke of the purpose of the gifts as the building up of the body:

> If we live by the truth and in love, we shall grow
> completely into Christ, who is the head by whom the
> whole Body is fitted and joined together, every joint
> adding its own strength, for each individual part to
> work according to its function. So the body grows until
> it has built itself up in love. (Ephesians 4:15-16 NJB)

Community is built up, then, and grows in health and wholeness through loving service to one another. When people lay down their lives for one another, and use the gifts that God has given them for each other's benefit, Christ becomes real in human flesh, and the incarnation continues in history. Then the experienced reality of being Christ together can be celebrated in liturgy.

In recent years, however, various liturgical experts have suggested that liturgy is the place to develop community and experience the presence of Christ in our midst. They know that Sunday Mass is the one time when the entire parish (or at least a good part of it) can get together to be taught what it means to be a faith community. From the earliest days of the liturgical renewal after Vatican II, they therefore encouraged parishes to put great emphasis on the liturgy, to encourage lay participation in reading and singing, to use the homily as a means of relating the scriptures to daily life, and to enhance the symbolism of the Mass with appropriate vestments, decorations and so on.

Now that we have been trying this approach for some

years in the Catholic Church, we see clearly that it has not reaped the fruits that were promised. To be sure, some parishes have beautiful liturgies, designed by hard-working committees, presented by well-trained leaders, enriched by very able musicians. But for many of our people, this is merely the English Sunday show which has replaced the Latin Sunday show. They attend, but they do not participate. They come in as strangers, shake hands with strangers at the sign of peace, and leave as strangers. They are not really a community. The education which was supposed to happen through the liturgy alone has by and large failed to happen.

Religious educators since Vatican II have likewise stressed teaching in the classroom as a way to communicate the meaning of the Church as the body of Christ. The idea here is to fill the students with the right beliefs, so that they know what Christian life and worship are all about when they come to Mass on Sunday. But the repeated failure of CCD programs shows clearly that much more is needed than the right beliefs, whether taught from a catechism or from a more contemporary book. Sometimes only a handful of kids show up for class on a weekday night, and they would not be there at all if their parents did not force them. Nor are Catholic schools much better. Sometimes when I tell high school students about New Jerusalem, I get the impression that they are hearing for the very first time about the Lord and the life that he offers them. Our young people have had their fill of beliefs and doctrines; they long for the experience of the Lord which can only be had in the body of Christ.

The advantage of a community such as New Jerusalem is that we come to meet the Lord in one another in many ways, long before we come together to celebrate his presence among us. We know each others' needs and failings, and we discover that we have the gifts to minister to them. We know each others' strengths and talents, and we can call forth their gifts to help build up the body. We meet together in small groups to pray and study the Bible, not because someone has told us we must, but because we feel the need to pray and to learn from the scriptures what the Lord wants to tell us. We come together once a week for a large, informal Eucharist where we really feel connected with the other members of the body and rejoice in what the Lord is doing in our midst.

From my own experience in a Christian community, I am convinced that we become the new creation that St. Paul speaks about only through a network of such relationships, living in a body of Christ. It does not happen in a momentary religious experience, as is sometimes suggested. Too many people who are "baptized in the Spirit" dry up and wither away, usually because their spiritual rebirth was not nourished and nurtured in an ongoing set of relationships. They become the dropouts of the various renewal movements, turned off by the very thought of what briefly turned them on.

In St. Paul's view, the Spirit is found not so much in individuals as in the body of believers who together have Christ as their head. In such an ongoing community, the Lord can work and the Spirit can grow in ways that individuals would never know on their own. We teach each other and are taught, we help each other and are helped, we forgive each other and are forgiven in ways that, when they happen, we know it is the Lord's doing and not our own. To serve one another, the Spirit gives us gifts we would never have discovered, were they not needed by other members of the body. And every time we think we've made it, the Lord shows us we don't really have it all together by challenging us with further personal and communal growth.

This is not to say there are no times of dullness and deadness, temptation and sin, jealously and ill will, fear and aloneness in a Christian community. That is, in fact, the norm! And that is why growth and conversion is almost forced upon us. In community life our weakness and our sinfulness are even more apparent than if we were all living private lives and could show only our best face to one another. Living together brings out not only the best in us but also the worst in us. But the miracle is that when we are in need of healing, the Lord is there to heal us, incarnate in the brothers and sisters who will pick us up and bind our wounds and be our salvation.

Jesus saves. We have heard those words in our own Catholic tradition and more recently from evangelical Christians. But according to St. Paul, and according to my own experience as a priest, as a Franciscan and as a member of a community such as New Jerusalem, Jesus saves us in and through a body of believers who are made one by his Spirit. To the degree that every parish, every prayer group, every school, every religious order, every assembly of the body of Christ is gathered in love, trusting in the Father, obedient to the gospel and open to the Spirit, Jesus saves. And the good news is that his salvation is not just for us individually, and not just for our own particular community, but through his continued incarnation, for all peoples, all races, religions and ways of life.

The Church is not so much the place where the converted gather, but the place where true conversion, surrender and universal love can happen. It is God's vehicle for the reconciliation and unity of all creation.

CHAPTER SIX

Apocalypse:
The New Jerusalem

The book which brings the Bible
to a close has traditionally been called the Apocalypse. In
modern translations, however, it is usually called Revelation.
The earlier name comes from a Greek word and the later name
comes from a Latin word, but both mean the same: to uncover
or unveil what is hidden. The Apocalypse is, therefore, a
revelation of something which has been hidden and which the
author describes in a series of dramatic and powerful images.

No book in the Bible has been given more interpretations
than the Revelation of John. Through the centuries many writers
have tried to explain its cryptic imagery and many of them have
claimed to have at last found the key to unlock its hidden
meaning. Usually this biblical book has been interpreted in a
very literal sense, with each image or sequence of images being
linked to real persons and events in history. Even today there
are some people who believe that by reading this book it is
possible to predict what will happen at the end of the world.

Modern scripture scholars, however, take a much
different approach. They point out that its very strangeness
should be a clue that we are dealing here with a type of mentality
and a form of literature which are very different from our own.
It is not a recent book written by a modern author who might
have wanted to conceal detailed knowledge behind a
complicated veil of images, as though it were a secret code that
needed to be broken. Rather this is a very ancient genre of
writing (of which there are other biblical and nonbiblical

examples) in which the author expresses a simple theme in sometimes fantastic imagery and symbolism.

If we were to express the theme of the Apocalypse in a single sentence, it would be something like: Steadfast faith in the midst of persecution is based on a sure hope of future glory. To say it yet another way: No matter how bad the conflict gets, good will triumph over evil at the end. Or to say it theologically: Even though Satan seems to be winning now, God's love and power will ultimately give the victory to Christ.

This book was written toward the end of the first century after persecutions of Christians by the emperors Nero and Domitian. And with Christianity still illegal in the Roman Empire, there was no end of conflict in sight, even though there were periods of respite between aggressive persecution. The forecast predicated more stormy weather before the skies would clear. Some Christians were perhaps beginning to doubt that the hurricane would ever pass. Not the author of the Apocalypse, however.

The author is a Christian prophet who gives his name as John, but the peculiarities of his writing style make it clear that he is not the same John as the author of the fourth gospel. It could have been written by St. John the Apostle or one of his disciples. Or it may even be that the book in its present form was composed by a "school" (that is, several writers) who attributed it to St. John because it was based on his prophetic visions. The author says that he received these visions from God while in exile on the island of Patmos off the western coast of Asia Minor (Revelation 1:9).

In the second and third chapters John addresses prophesies to seven Churches at the western end of Asia Minor with whom he had suffered in the recent persecutions. The excitement of the first years of Christianity, when it had been spreading like wildfire, was dampened. The initial hope for the return of Christ during the lifetime of the first generation of Christians was dimmed. Yet hope still remained for those with faith. Those who believed that Jesus' way of living led to eternal life still trusted that the Father would ultimately vindicate his Son.

The Apocalypse, then, is written in the midst of struggle,

to Christians who are experiencing struggle, about the meaning and the outcome of that struggle. Throughout the book there is a constant war being waged between good and evil. The war is all around them, and so the images the author uses to describe it are drawn on a gigantic scale. Angels and dragons battle in the heavens. Storms rage across the sky, stars fall and mountains are shattered. Wars and plagues and famines scorch the earth killing countless thousands. The cosmic drama symbolizes the very worst that was happening and was still likely to happen.

If Paul had written to those Churches, he might have said that the body of Christ was being crucified in the world, enduring the sufferings of Jesus in hope of resurrection. John has that same vision, but he describes it in a much more ancient and middle-eastern fashion, using fantastic and kaleidoscopic imagery. He realizes that what happened in Jesus is continuing in the incarnate Christ. And so his prophetic insight sees that after the passion must come resurrection. Because the Father raised up Jesus from the dead, God will likewise save those who live in Christ.

In this respect, John is much like the prophets of ancient Israel. Like them, he beholds past, present and future in a single flash of insight. He looks into the past and sees the pattern of God's action. He looks at the present and sees the same pattern at work. And he looks into the future and sees the divine pattern continuing. Then he speaks to the present with the conviction that what God did is what God is doing and will continue to do. God does not change; it is only we who change. God is ever faithful to his promises, and since he has already begun to fulfill his promise of eternal life by raising Jesus, Christians need only to wait upon God for the salvation which will surely come.

A Unique Literary Style

Strictly speaking, however, Revelation is not a prophetic book written in the standard prophetic genre of the Old Testament. Even less is it a book containing prophetic utterances in the sense of specific predictions. It is written in a very special style called "apocalyptic." We must see this clearly if we are to understand the Book of Revelation and not misinterpret it.

The apocalyptic style presents all the events taking place in the panorama of the world as though we are looking from heaven at the unfolding of a spectacular drama. We are given a vision from the perspective of eternity, a perspective which is often needed when we are so caught up in our immediate problems. The author is trying to show that God is bigger than any of our problems, and so he calls us to that larger vision which faith in God offers us.

One literary technique which the author employs to do this (and it is a technique which is common in apocalyptic literature) is to write the whole story in the past tense: This happened, then this happened, then this happened, etc. It gives the appearance of past history, as though everything described has already taken place.

We see the same thing in the visions of some of the Old Testament prophets. They saw the downfall of Israel or the return from exile (depending on when they were writing) as surely as if it had already happened. This apocalyptic perspective can give the appearance that, from the perspective of eternity, God looks back on future events and sees everything that will happen. It therefore appears that everything is predetermined and that there is nothing we can do to alter the course of events. This is not, however, the author's intent.

Here John sees the end of persecution and the ultimate triumph of God as surely as if it had already happened. And he does so, not to make people resigned to the inevitable, but to inspire them to courageous faith in God's power to conquer the forces of evil.

The apocalyptic literary genre is well suited for presenting the meaning of history, for it describes the human drama on a cosmic scale. Humanity is stumbling forward, surrounded by the storm of events, trying to achieve happiness and peace. It works against terrific odds, encountering setbacks that often make human progress seem like two steps forward and three steps backward. But because the risen Christ is the Lord of history and because the power of the incarnate God is unconquerable, the progress of humanity toward salvation is assured. In Christ the victory is already won, and the sign of this victory is the resurrection. Still, it is not a human achievement; it is a divine gift, just as the raising of Jesus was.

From the earliest chapters of the Bible we see humanity in turmoil, deluged by its own wickedness, deluded by pride, beleaguered by antagonism, confused by its many failed attempts to conquer heaven and become like God. The dim memory of paradise lost urges generation after generation to try to create for themselves an ordered society. Yet it is always by God's power that humankind makes any progress at all. In the Israelite kingdom, God's power even succeeds in founding a city which David named Jerusalem, which means "city of peace."

Although established through divine providence, the earthly Jerusalem is destroyed when it forsakes its Lord and relies on human strength. Through God's forgiveness it is rebuilt, but it never becomes the paradise of peace that humanity is seeking. Nevertheless, it remains a symbol of hope, a sign of what the human race is blindly stumbling toward.

Thus, in the last chapters of the Apocalypse, Jerusalem appears again. But it is not a city built by human hands. It is a city of God that comes down from the heavens and is bestowed on humanity as gift. It is God's gift of peace, which is not a human achievement but a fulfillment of divine promise. God's victory is absolute grace. God's peace is a gift of eternal love. Paradise is regained in precisely the same way that it was orginally given—as gift.

The new Jerusalem is a symbol of that perfectly ordered society in which God and humanity are in right relationship. It is the kingdom where God reigns and where people live in harmony with one another. It is the city of peace, where God's love is finally and fully incarnate upon the earth. It is the home of the body of Christ, given to those who are anointed with his Spirit. As it is announced from the heavens: "The kingdom of the world now belongs to the Lord and his Anointed, and he will reign for ever and ever" (Revelation 11:15).

But that is only the final symbol in a book which is rampant with symbolism. The number seven, sacred to the ancients as symbolizing the union of heaven and earth, appears over and over again: seven earthly cities, seven sealed scrolls, seven trumpet blasts and seven bowls of plagues. Christ is depicted as the Son of Man, the Lamb of God, the King of Kings, the Bridegroom of the Church. Humanity is represented as the people and the nations of the earth, as the angels who are faithful to the Lamb, as the saints in heaven who sing the praise of God, and by the woman who brings Christ into the world. In chapter 12, her child is taken into heaven and, from there, wages constant war against the evil which attacks the woman and her other children.

In this kaleidoscope of symbolism, it is not always possible to fix stable meanings to the images. Sometimes the woman is Mary, sometimes she is the persecuted Church. Sometimes Christ is Jesus, sometimes he is the victorious Church. Likewise the symbols of evil tumble into one another, representing heavenly and earthly forces of destruction. The four horsemen wreaking havoc on the earth, the sea dragon with seven heads, the two-horned beast from the earth, the gods Gog and Magog—all these and more stand for one and then another of the enemies of God. The harlot city, Babylon, represents not only Rome but every place of prostitution, debauchery and idolatry which, in the end, will be thrown into the sea and replaced by the holy city, Jerusalem, which will descend from the heavens and cover all the earth.

Although battle after battle wages through the book, although famine and pestilence scourge, although death and destruction rage, the end is never in doubt. From God's viewpoint, it is all past tense. The victory has already been won; it needs only to be revealed in full. Thus the opposing camps of good and evil are never equal. There is never any danger that Satan will triumph and Christ will be defeated, no matter how terrible or successful a persecution may appear. That is why apocalyptic literature has the power to console and give hope in impossible times.

A Vision of What Really Is

In his own way, then, John is writing the equivalent of a good old-fashioned western for the Christian pioneers of the first century. He is saying that no matter how many redskins and bandits attack their wagon train, the cavalry will eventually appear and rescue them. And no matter how many storms and droughts they travel through, they are sure to reach a land of peace and plenty. But to get there, they need lots of faith and hope.

He writes this way because some Christians in Asia Minor were beginning to doubt. Perhaps some had set out on the journey of faith unaware of the dangers and not expecting any hardships. So John reveals to them the deeper faith which a perilous journey demands. He encourages them to outstare the darkness and walk steady in the wind. And he reminds them that regardless of the way things look, God has revealed in Jesus the way things really are.

In this respect John is doing for his community what Don Quixote does for Aldonza in *Man of La Mancha*. Others call her a worthless prostitute, but he refuses to accept their definition of reality. Day after day he addresses her as the pure Dulcinea, and he insists that she is a beautiful and worthy lady. At last the power of his affirmation overcomes her disbelief, and she becomes what he had really seen in her.

By the early Church's acceptance of John's masterpiece as the inspired word of God, it affirmed that his vision of reality is valid for Christians of every age. The power of the word of God is that it reveals reality to us, even when the world around us looks very different. More importantly, it speaks the truth to us about ourselves, even when we think we are something different. We may think we are worthless, but God tells us we are precious. We may think we are abandoned, but God tells us we are his children. We may think we are going nowhere, but God tells us that everything we ever dreamed of is already ours, if we would only open our eyes and see it.

Yet it is not only we who speak the untruth to ourselves. Our culture tells us we have to make it on our own, and if we do not have what the world counts as success we must be failures. Even religion has often condemned us, telling us that we are sinners who have to earn our own salvation or suffer the consequences. But the redemptive word of God tells us we are created in God's image and calls us to be re-created in the likeness of Christ.

From creation to re-creation, it is all God's work. At creation, the world was like clay in God's hands, shaped into the natural pattern of divine goodness. The re-creation of humanity is the reshaping of our spirit in the pattern of the Holy Spirit, making us children of God and brothers and sisters of Jesus. That is where the world and we are headed, that is where the Lord is leading us. And so the Apocalypse describes the grand finale of God's eternally creating and re-creating love:

> Then the former heaven and the earth with its dangerous seas passed away, and I beheld a new heaven and a new earth. The holy city, new Jerusalem, came out of God's heaven, beautiful as a bride prepared to meet her husband. I heard a loud voice call from the throne, "Behold, the home of God is now for every child of the earth. He shall dwell among them, and they shall be his people. He shall be their God, forever with them. He shall wipe every tear from their eyes, and death shall be no more. Neither shall there be any mourning or grieving, for the former world has passed away." Then the one who sat upon the throne said, "Look! I am making all things new!" (Revelation 21:1-5a)

We must remember, though, that the prophet is not describing a vision of the future. From God's perspective there is neither future nor past; eternity is eternally present here and now. The divine pattern is always the same, God's love is always real, and the word of God is always true. Thus John continues:

> And he said to me, "Write all this down, for what I am telling you is trustworthy and true. It is already done. For I am the Alpha and the Omega, the A and the Z, the beginning and the end." (Revelation 21:5b-6)

Thus Christ is proclaimed as the center of history, surrounded from beginning to end by God's redemptive love. There is no need to seek the Lord elsewhere, because he is already dwelling among us. There is no place that we can go to

162

find his love, because it is always being given to us right where we are. God is loving creation into existence, and the Spirit is at work re-creating those who open their hearts to the power of God's love.

To be filled with that love is to be one with Jesus. To be filled with that love is to be in the body of Christ at the center of history. To be filled with that love is to look at the world from God's perspective, to see how beautiful it is, and to behold how glorious it is becoming.

Sometimes it is only prophets and poets who see that. But if they describe their vision for us, we too receive their revelation. Their insight shows us what is really real, and it prepares us to see it for ourselves. The prophet John did that for the Church in his day, and in doing that he shared his vision with the Church in all ages. The poet Gerard Manley Hopkins described that same reality for his day in "God's Grandeur," inviting us to behold the glory that is all around us:

> The world is charged with the grandeur of God.
>   It will flame out, like shining from shook foil;
>   It gathers to a greatness, like the ooze of oil
> Crushed. Why do men then now not reck his rod?
>
> Generations have trod, have trod, have trod;
>   And all is seared with trade; bleared, smeared with
>   toil;
>   And wears man's smudge and shares man's smell;
>   the soil
> Is bare now, nor can foot feel, being shod.
>
> And for all this, nature is never spent;
>   There lives the dearest freshness deep down things;
> And though the last lights of the black West went
>   Oh, morning, at the brown brink eastward,
>   springs—
> Because the Holy Ghost over the bent
>   World broods with warm breast and with ah! bright
>   wings.

To have the vision of faith is to see that the ordinary is

in fact extraordinary, that the secular is sacred, and the Lord is in the midst of the world redeeming it. To experience that is to know God.

CONCLUSION

Our New Jerusalem:
A Modern Faith Journey

Throughout these two volumes on the great themes of scripture, I have been insisting that I can vouch for what I say not just because I have read it in the Bible but because I have experienced the truth of God's word in my own life. From time to time in these chapters I have given you examples from the life of our community, New Jerusalem, but now it might be good to do even more than that.

The Bible closes with the image of the new Jerusalem coming down from heaven. This apocalyptic language can seem far removed from real life, even though it is beautifully poetic. So to help make what the scriptures are talking about more real for you, I'd like to round out these lessons on the Bible with a rather down-to-earth description of the New Jerusalem I haved lived in, and how it came to be.

Just before being ordained I was asked what I would like to do in my ministry, and I said I really wanted to preach the word of God to adults, perhaps by giving missions and retreats in the Franciscan tradition. If I could not do that, then my second and third preferences would be to teach scriptural theology or to work with the Indians in New Mexico. The one thing I was sure I did not want to do was work with teenagers. But the Lord had different plans. My order needed someone to teach at Roger Bacon High School in Cincinnati, and I agreed to go if it would be for only one year. That was January of 1971, and I still felt pretty much like running my own life.

In June I went home to Topeka, Kansas, to be ordained

165

a priest in the parish where I had grown up. After so many years of study and training the great day had finally arrived, but for some reason it did not feel as exciting as I had expected it to. In fact, I was feeling sort of numb, and even when the bishop laid his hands on me to ordain me, it seemed I was barely aware of what was going on.

I remember, though, that when the ceremony was over, I went back to the vestibule of the church where all my relatives and friends had gathered. One by one they came to congratulate me, with the bishop standing on one side and my beaming parents on the other.

Then a woman I didn't know came up to me and said, "Father, I want to talk to you."

"My gosh, a counseling call already!" I thought. I felt like saying, "Can't you see that this is my big moment? Why can't you come back later?" But instead, I said something a little more polite.

Undeterred, the woman said it was important, so I excused myself and went with her to the less-crowded side of the vestibule. She looked at me and said, "You are going to be used by the Holy Spirit." I felt that was no big news, since I was a priest now. But she went on. "You probably don't know this, but you're standing on the spot where many people say the pentecostal movement started in 1900. On January 1, in a little building that was sometimes called 'Stone's Folly,' a group of people met to pray and ask for the gifts of the Spirit. They kept meeting and praying for a full year, and then, on New Year's Eve, the Holy Spirit touched them in a powerful way. They began to speak in tongues and to experience healings and many of the things that St. Paul speaks about, but which had been unheard of for centuries. They began to share what had happened to them with others, and though many called them foolish and crazy, they realized that God had given them the same gifts that they had read about in the New Testament.

"A few decades later, the old building in which they had met was torn down. This Catholic church on the corner of 17th and Stone was put up on that spot. But you're the first priest to be ordained here. While I was attending your Mass the Lord told me you are going to be used in a special way for his work."

I thanked her, and although I didn't really understand all that she was saying, I guess in some sense I wanted to believe her. In the busyness of everything that followed, I forgot all about that meeting. But then, when I got back to Cincinnati and started teaching at Roger Bacon, strange things started happening which reminded me of that woman and her prophecy. Somehow, through what I was saying in the classroom and at school Masses, kids were being touched by a spirit that they hadn't felt before. Even sophomore boys felt it, and they're the toughest audience that anyone could ever face. As one of them said to me, "Obviously, it's not you, Father Rohr!" That took me down a notch or two, but I knew he was right.

I learned that even high school students were ready to hear the Lord and follow him in a deeper way. Some of them began to stay after school, and even come around on weekends. We would talk a lot about Jesus and what it meant to be a Christian, and a few of us began to pray together. It brought us closer to the Lord and to each other every time we did it.

In the middle of the school year, I was asked to take over the youth retreats for the Archdiocese of Cincinnati. I said that I would do it, because by this time I could see that the Lord was leading me to minister to young people. Six months before nothing could have convinced me to work with teenagers, but here I was volunteering to preach retreats for high school students.

I had to leave in the middle of the first retreat for boys to attend a CFM (Catholic Family Movement) convention on the other side of town. I wound up speaking to that group much longer than I had planned and got back to the retreat very late and very hoarse. When I arrived, I could see that the boys had gotten nowhere in my absence. It was as though most of them had not heard anything that I had asked them to think about. I had talked about community, but it was clear that there was no sense of community at the retreat. Everyone was just doing his own thing, and some of them were getting rowdy.

I still had to give the main talk for that day on the love of the Father. I felt that the good news of Jesus had to get through to them somehow if the retreat was going to have any effect on them at all. So I asked the three young men who were with me from Roger Bacon to pray with me about the situation. I knew that these three had come to know the Lord, and I felt I needed their support.

The four of us went into a small room next to where the others were goofing off. Right away one of them said to me, "Father, you've always taught us to trust the Lord. Now we're telling you to trust the Lord. You're going to go out there and preach, and we're going to pray while you do it. And we'll trust the Lord that they're going to hear what God wants them to hear." Another one opened the Bible to that passage where Paul says that the Lord uses our weakness to show his own strength (2 Corinthians 12:9-10). So we claimed that word as meant for us. Then I went into the other room to preach, while they stayed and prayed.

Something happened that night which I'll never forget. After I finished preaching, I invited anyone who wanted to go to Confession to come down to my room. Many more came than I had expected, and most of them were radiant with a joy that they could not explain. A short while before they had been typical high school seniors, but something new had happened to them. Something had touched them, something had changed them, and it was obviously not me.

After two hours of this, listening to them try to tell me what they had experienced, the last boy left my room. I went ouside to get some fresh air. Usually a bunch of them would be out on the grounds, but there was no one there. I went over to the hall where we usually had our snacks, but it was dark and silent. I looked all around, and in desperation I even looked in the chapel.

I opened the door—and there they were, all of them, kneeling around the altar. Some were reading their Bibles. One was playing a guitar quietly. Some had their arms around one another. Others had tears in their eyes. A few were praying in a strange, unknown language. I fell to my knees and began to pray. I knew that what I had witnessed was the work of the Lord.

The next few weeks I sometimes wondered if my superiors were going to quickly grant my earlier request and send me to New Mexico! There was a lot of misunderstanding going around about what had happened on the retreat. The boys had gone back to their schools like fireballs, and nothing could keep them from telling other kids about what they had experienced. Some of the teachers who heard about it were afraid that the retreat master had used some psychological gimmick to mess up the kids' heads—or worse.

The boys who came back to visit me, however, assured me that what they had discovered that night was the most real thing in their lives. They were worried about losing it, and they wanted to keep it. So I asked them who had given it to them, and they were sure it was the Lord. "All right," I said, "if this is just a people-trip, it won't last. But if it's really a God-trip as you say, we'll have to pray together and see where it goes from here."

They all agreed to come that Friday to the friary where I lived. There were so many of them that they filled the front parlor, and we must have prayed and sang for three solid hours. We celebrated a joyful Eucharist together. Sometimes they sang so loud I thought the ceiling would fall down! I learned the next day that some of the other friars were not too happy about all the noise, and again I thought I would be sent to the Indian reservation.

But the Lord, in his wisdom, was taking care of everything in a way that I couldn't even begin to keep track of. Things just seemed to happen, although nothing seemed terribly important in itself. I wondered if maybe I was just fooling myself, giving the credit to God. Maybe at some deeper level I was really manipulating it all, and didn't even know it. Maybe I was just doing my own thing, and not being honest enough to admit it.

Some people certainly thought that. They said I was a teenage priest founding a teenage parish. So a board was appointed to investigate what I was preaching and to find out what was behind it. In some sense I welcomed that, because it took the burden off my shoulders, and I was willing to submit what I was doing to the judgment of the Church. So as the Lord would have it, it all worked out. The investigating committee saw that everything I was preaching had a foundation in the scriptures. And even though they had some reservations, they allowed me to go ahead with the youth retreat program.

At the same time the number of kids coming on Friday nights continued to grow. I'm sure a lot of them came for the wrong reasons—and after a while they stopped coming. But there was a remnant, and it formed the core of the larger group. They really learned about the Lordship and love of Christ, giving of their time and energy to so many others and laying their lives down for one another.

Today we look back on those first months and call them our "zap days." We were seeing fireworks all the time. Every prayer meeting seemed to produce a new conversion. We couldn't wait until the next Friday to see what the Lord would do next, getting kids off drugs, producing healings, bringing reconciliations. We saw so many miracles and so many transformed lives. But that's what God sometimes does at the beginning, to strengthen your faith and call you to an even deeper faith.

It wasn't long before we could no longer all fit in that front room of the friary. Someone in another part of town invited us to use her house, which gave us a little more room. But the same thing happened all over again. Our numbers grew, and when we sang the floor would sag from the weight of the crowd swaying and clapping. I said to myself, "It's time to see the bishop."

Claiming a House for the Lord

I made an appointment to see Archbishop Leibold on February 7, 1972. We prayed together before I went to see him, asking the Lord to give us some indication about what to expect. Not one but three people in our group opened their Bibles to the same verses in the Book of Chronicles, an obscure passage suggesting that a house would be given to us, and that everything we needed would be prepared for us. The final line was, "The officials and all the people are entirely at your command" (See 1 Chronicles 28:20-21). We felt for sure that God had given us an answer, and from then on I didn't worry at all. In my heart I knew that the bishop would be behind us.

When I got to see the bishop, I decided to tell him the

whole story. I told him what I had done and what I thought about what was happening. I talked about religious education, prayer and scripture, liturgies and sermons, everything I thought needed to be said. He probably got tired of listening to me!

Finally I said, "Now this is going to sound conceited, but if you can get us a house, I promise that the Lord can reach more kids through it than three of your high schools put together—and for one hundredth the cost. But I don't have any money. The Franciscans haven't given me any, and the diocese hasn't given me any. But we've learned to trust the Lord. I know he's leading us."

Archbishop Leibold said simply, "Father, somehow I believe you." And he went out himself that night, driving around Cincinnati, trying to find us a house.

In the weeks after that meeting with the bishop, every possibility fell through for one reason or another. Some people didn't want teenagers around; they were afraid we'd tear up the property. Some houses would have taken too much money to fix up, and I didn't have any. But we continued to pray, claiming the promise of the Lord that he would give us a house. The weeks turned into months, but we did not give up hope.

Then on May 15th I heard about a mansion. It was the old Crosley estate, built by a man who had made Crosley radios. A few of us went out to take a look at it, and we felt at once it would be perfect. It was located in a small wooded area in a beautiful part of Cincinnati, just right for retreats. We buzzed around looking in the windows, and when we thought we'd seen enough, we stopped by the front door to pray. Above the door we saw the Crosley family crest with the Latin inscription, *Confido per crucem*—"I trust in the cross!"

I have no idea why Powell Crosley picked that motto for his family, but we claimed it as our own. We said, "Okay, Lord, we trust in the cross, too! We claim this house for you." And we went home, confident that he wanted it for us to do his work.

The mansion was owned by a nearby Catholic hospital, so I went to see the administrator to see what could be done. I was just as bold and forthright with him as I had been with the bishop: "I'd like to have that house. I have no money, but I can work visiting patients if you want me to."

The administrator was sympathetic but unmoved. "Well, Father," he said, "it's unlikely that we can let you use it. As you see, it's a valuable old Tudor mansion. Your teenagers would probably carve their initials in the paneling and do other things to lessen the property's value. But I'll give you the same chance that everyone else has. Early in June there will be a committee meeting to see who gets the mansion. Other groups are asking for it, and just between you and me they're more likely to get it." I thanked him for his time, but I left with a feeling of "Don't call me; I'll call you."

I told the kids what had happened, so we prayed and claimed the promise of the Lord. Then on June 1, Archbishop Leibold died suddenly and unexpectedly. Some of the kids were discouraged because although he had been behind us, we felt that a lot of the pastors weren't. Were we going to get any support from the Church? We didn't know who our new bishop might be. We had many people praying for us, but not many of them were Church officials.

One nun who had been with us from the beginning prayed throughout the night for us. The next day she called me and said, "Richard, you're sure to get the house because the Archbishop is with the Lord." I thought to myself that she was just being sisterly and supportive. I did not really believe her, although I wanted to. I was sort of in-between, thinking that if it worked out, I would know the Lord had done it, but if it didn't—well, I did not want to be too disappointed. But the kids believed with all their hearts that the house would be ours!

On June 7 I went to Archbishop Leibold's funeral, and when I got home there was a message for me saying that the house was ours. Our prayer had been answered just as we had hoped! The mansion would be lent to us at absolutely no cost until the hospital needed it for something else. All our utility bills would be paid and the furnishings we needed provided. The prophecy had been fulfilled!

In that house I experienced more joy and community than I had thought was possible in this life. We made the Crosleys' master bedroom into a chapel and called it the Upper Room, and in that one room alone I witnessed more works of power and love than I had ever hoped to see in my entire priesthood. Every night the young people would come and we would pray late into the night. Very often our prayer would naturally lead into a Mass which would last for hours. The Lord was teaching us in so many ways what it means to be a community and how to be a community.

We were babies in the Spirit then, if I might use that term. The Lord knew we could not manage a place on our own, so he spoiled us. Everything was literally handed to us! We were the spoiled brats of God, but we didn't mind it one bit! We lived in the radiance of his smile for months that seemed like years, since each week was filled with so many blessings and surprises.

But then, on January 29, I was praying alone in the Upper Room. I can still see the sun streaming in the window, pouring onto the red rug. At one point, it seemed the Lord was telling me, "Richard, you're not trusting me the way you used to. You're worrying about the kids and their problems. You're worrying about your own problems, too. Well, I gave you this place and I'm going to take it away. It's not your work; I'm just using you. So cool it, and learn to rest in me again."

When something like that comes to you in prayer, you're not sure whether the Lord is really speaking to you. Maybe they're just your own thoughts, even though you think they're coming from God. So I said, "Lord, if you are trying to tell me something, give me a sign in scripture." Now, that's a very untheological thing to do, I admit. Charismatics sometimes open the Bible at random and expect the Lord to talk to them through it. I'd be a fool to recommended it to everyone in every circumstance, but I'd be denying my own experience if I said that it could never happen. So I opened to the Second Book of Maccabees, and when I looked at the page I read:

> However, the Lord had not chosen the people for the sake of the place, but the place for the sake of the people. (2 Maccabees 5:19 JB)

At the time, I did not know if that had any real significance, or if I was just playing Bible roulette. I closed the book and went to my room. Not more than five minutes later the phone rang. The secretary of the hospital administrator was on the line, and she asked me if I could make an appointment Tuesday morning at 11 o'clock. I said simply, "Thank you. I'll be there."

As I put the phone down, I sensed the unmistakable presence of the Lord. I felt the most exhilarating joy and peace, even though I knew that the hospital was going to tell us that we had to leave the mansion. I knew how much the kids loved every brick of that old house, and how much it meant to all of us. But the most important thing was knowing that the Lord was with us. That's all that mattered. And since he was leading us, he would not lead us out of this place unless he had another prepared for us.

The following days I felt the presence of the Lord so intensely that it was impossible for me to worry about the future. When I went to talk with the administrator, I said, "I know you called me here about taking away the mansion. That's all right." And I shared with him about the word of the Lord which had come to me, and about the way we had all come to trust in the power of the Lord to find a new place for us.

"At the same time," I explained, "we Franciscans are not supposed to be ashamed to beg, and so I want to beg you to let us have it until Easter. We have retreats scheduled every weekend from now till then." The administrator said the hospital could wait that long, but no more.

That night when the kids gathered at the house, I said, "I'm going to tell you something, and after I tell it to you, promise me you'll say, 'Praise the Lord!'" They said they would. So I told them, "The Lord gives and the Lord takes away. Blessed be the name of the Lord! We have to leave the mansion." Their faces fell, but they managed to mumble, "Praise the Lord."

We began to pray together and to remind each other what we had been saying about the journey of faith. We remembered that when Israel was being led out of slavery, the people often wanted to stop and stay put, but Moses would call them to trust the Lord and believe in the land the Lord he had promised to give them. That's what the journey of faith is all about. The Lord is always calling us to a new land. He always wants to give us something more, and he wants to give it to us free.

Soon after that I went to see Archbishop Bernardin, who had just been appointed to Cincinnati. I told him what the Lord had been doing in our lives, and he said he would make good on Archbishop Leibold's promise to make sure we had a house. The kids all imagined that just before the deadline we would get a dramatic phone call from the bishop announcing that he'd found a new place for us, but it never came.

On Holy Saturday we had our last big liturgy in the mansion. The kids were packed from wall to wall. There was no longer room for all who came. For me, that was another confirmation that the Lord knew what he was doing by telling us we had to leave there.

I had a strong feeling that the Lord was going to give me a special gospel that night, so I did not use the usual lectionary. When it came time to read the gospel, I took the Bible from a girl standing next to me and threw it open. I put my eyes down and read the first passage that I looked at:

Do not let your hearts be troubled.
Trust in God still, and trust in me.
There are many rooms in my Father's house;
if there were not, I should have told you.
I am going now to prepare a place for you,
and after I have gone and prepared a place,
I shall return and take you with me,
so that where I am you may be too. (John 14:1-3a JB)

You could have scraped us off the ceiling! Everyone cried with joy because we knew the Lord was leading us to a new place, a place he was preparing for us. We all loved the mansion, and yet at the same time we had felt a little uneasy about living there—me especially, being a Franciscan. The kids had sometimes teased me about that. There were already some of them who felt we should be living among the poor.

On Easter Sunday the core group and I celebrated a glorious sunrise Mass together. But we didn't have a new house. So I moved out and we stored whatever belonged to the community. The young people waited and trusted and prayed. Then, about a month later, Archbishop Bernardin called to say that the diocese was closing a school in Winton Place and that if we wanted it, we could have it.

Right away we drove down to that neighborhood and took a look at it. The setting was not a wooded estate, and it was not a mansion. The school and the convent next to it were pretty torn up, and a lot of houses in the area were either run down or boarded up. The school alone had 42 broken windows. We knew it would take a lot of work to fix it up so we could use it for retreats and liturgies, but for a year now the Lord had been showing us that we could work together. The convent too would take a lot of doing, since it was 125 years old, but we could see that it would give us space of our own to fix up and do things that we never could have done in the mansion. And we knew the Lord was leading us to that poorer part of town, to be a sign there of his love. So I told the bishop, "Yes, we'd be honored to have it."

Making the Lord's New Mansion

On June 7, exactly a year to the day that I had received word that the Crosley mansion would be lent to us, we moved into Winton Place. On June 10, the feast of Pentecost, we had our first Mass there, and I asked those who came if they would volunteer to make this the Lord's new mansion.

The next day the young people started coming with buckets and rags and sandpaper and scrapers. Slowly the buildings began to be transformed. Everything was done by teenagers—the cleaning and the painting, the patching and the plastering, even the plumbing and the wiring. And through it all we continued to pray and trust and wait upon the Lord. In the course of time he also gave us the name for our community: New Jerusalem. (Presumptuous, weren't we!)

For a while we continued to meet on Friday nights in a Catholic high school gym in order to accommodate the large crowds who continued to come to the community prayer meetings. Eventually, though, the Lord led us to center more of our activity in that neighborhood. The prayer meetings and liturgies are now held in the remodeled gym of the old school

176

which, in a Francisican spirit, we named the *Portiuncula*, the "little portion." Some of us live in the convent, but some have also moved into other houses in the area.

When we pray together now, we don't always see fireworks any more. The Lord seems to be leading us on a deeper journey of faith, purifying a remnant, teaching us how to love one another. But always he is at the center of our life together. He is the head of this living body of Christ.

The early Church called Jesus the messiah, the anointed one. But now the anointing is upon the community. The body of Christ is anointed with the Spirit of God, which we have learned from our own experience is a Spirit of power. In and through us, God has done things that we would never have thought possible. God's spirit is also the Spirit of love, and we know now that that is not an abstract concept but a tangible reality. It is also a Spirit of prayer, which enables us to thank God for bringing us to where we are and leading us to where we don't yet know. But we don't have to worry about that.

The only thing that matters is that we know who is leading us. The Lord is creating our lives anew, creating us together as a people, and so we are being saved as a people. In teaching us how to love and trust one another, he teaches us how to love and trust him. And in teaching us how to love and trust him, he teaches us how to love and trust one another.

That's the journey of faith. Little by little, the Lord becomes as evident to you as the other people around you. Little by little, what the scriptures speak about becomes as real as wood that you can touch, and as real as ground that you can walk upon. You get to know what the Bible is talking about, not so much because you have studied the scriptures as a scholar, but because you have lived the life of Jesus as a disciple, as a member of his body.

There are always some who doubt that reality. There always have been, and there always will be. Many are called but few are chosen. The way into the kingdom is by a narrow gate. In these and other images the scriptures tell us that although the life of the Spirit is meant for everyone, not everyone believes and chooses it.

For our God is a God of freedom. He leaves us free to

live in a hut of our own making, or to live in the mansion he has prepared for us. He leaves us free to live in Egypt, or to follow him to the promised land. He leaves us free to live in slavery, or to answer his call to liberation across the desert. He leaves us free to live in isolation, or in community with members of the body of Christ. He leaves us free to live by our own power, or by the power of the Spirit who raised Jesus from the dead.

But if you let God be God, you will not be disappointed. No one who trusts in the Lord is put to shame. As the Book of Revelation teaches us, the battles we see going on around us do not matter in the end, for the victory is already won. It was won in Jesus, the Alpha and Omega of God's salvation. It is being won in Christ, wherever his body is empowered by his Spirit. And it will be won in the Lord, as all history becomes salvation history. Such is the graciousness of God.